SHOULD DRUGS BE LEGALIZED?

Definitely Out of the question Are you kidding
On no account Uh-huh Yes But Not in a million years
Not by a long shot Why not? Nope Certainly not By all means
Out of the question Yeah Not on your life Certain
y no means Unsure Under no circumstances Nay Maybe Unsu
ot in a million years Perhaps Nah Right on Don't kno
finitely Huh-uh Aye Forget it Not by a long shot Huh-uh Are you kiddi
Forget it Never But Out of the question Indeed Of cours
Uh-huh Certainly You bet On no account W
ossib Naturally Absolutely Sure Absolutely not Huh-uh Unsu
By no means Maybe Not in a million years Under no circumstanc
ay Unsure What if Never Certainly not Perhaps Absolutely no
What if Why not? Doubtful Not by a long shot Oka
rtainly not Certainly Out of the question Of course Absolutely
Definitely Why not? On no account Yes Are you kiddi
bsolutely not What if Nope Certainly not But By all mea
Uh-huh Indeed Absolutely not No Don't care No wa
y no means Unsure Under no circumstances Nay Maybe Unsu
Not in a million years Perhaps Nah Right on Yeah What if Mayl
Definitely Aye Forget it Huh-uh Of course Forget it Ye
h-huh Never But Not by a long shot Certainl
On no account Perhaps Out of the question Sure Yes Huh-uh Uns
Possibly Naturally Absolutely Nope Not in a million years Indee
Nay Unsure Maybe By all means Under no circumstanc
Nope But Never Certainly not Perhaps Why? Absolutely n
rtainly not Why not? Doubtful Not by a long shot Not on
What if But Indeed Not on your life But Of course Absolutely n
Definitely Certainly On no account Yes Are you kiddin
Forget it Why not? Certainly no By all mea
Absolutely not Don't care By no means Sure Not on
h-huh Doubtful Never No Perhaps
no means Unsure Under no circumstances Nay Maybe Unsu
Not in a million years Right on Yeah Certainly
Definitely Aye But Forget it Not by a long shot Huh-uh Don't know
rget it Never Out of the question What if Indeed Of course Are you kidding
Uh-huh Certain Sure You bet On no account Of course
ossibly Naturally Nope Not in a million years Huh-uh Unsu
By no means Maybe Nay Unsure By all means Under no circumstanc
What if But Never Certainly not Perhaps
ah Perhaps Why not? Not by a long

SHOULD DRUGS BE LEGALIZED?

TED GOTTFRIED

AUSTIN BRYN
5615 W. RACE AVE
CHICAGO, ILLINOIS 60644

TWENTY-FIRST CENTURY BOOKS
BROOKFIELD, CONNECTICUT

Photographs courtesy of Corbis: p. 14 (© James Marshall), 22 (© Jeffrey L. Rotman), 71 (© Todd Gipstein), 74 (© Annie Griffiths Belt), 89 (AFP), 93 (© Owen Franken); UPI/Corbis-Bettmann: p. 16; SuperStock: pp. 19, 36 (Culver Pictures); © DEA: p. 21; © 1998 Thor Swift/Impact Visual: p.26; Reuters/Corbis-Bettmann: p. 28; © CNS Productions: p. 31; New York Public Library Picture Collection: pp. 44, 48; Liaison Agency: pp. 51 (Library of Congress), 54, 60 (© Cynthia Johnson), 63 (© Deborah Copaken), 96 (© Antonio Ribeiro)

Library of Congress Cataloging-in-Publication Data
Gottfried, Ted.
Should drugs be legalized? / Ted Gottfried.
p. cm.
Includes bibliographical references and index.
Summary: Provides a history of drug use and abuse, presents cases for legalization, decriminalization, and other drug policy reforms, as well as the case for strengthening existing drug policy, and examines policies in other countries.
ISBN 0-7613-1314-1 (lib. bdg.)
1. Drug legalization—United States Juvenile literature. 2. Narcotics, Control of—United States Juvenile literature. 3. Drug abuse—United States Juvenile literature. 4. Narcotic laws—United States Juvenile literature. [1. Drug legalization. 2. Drug abuse. 3. Narcotic laws.] I. Title.
HV5825.G677   2000
362.29'0973—dc21   99-31163   CIP

Published by Twenty-First Century Books
A Division of The Millbrook Press, Inc.
2 Old New Milford Road
Brookfield, Connecticut 06804
www.millbrookpress.com

Many thanks to Dan, Loraine, and Jonathan Gottfried and Rudy and Melanie Kornmann for their patience, help, and advice with the many computer problems I encountered while writing this book. My gratitude also to Janet Bode and to the personnel of the New York Central Research Library, the Mid-Manhattan Library, and especially the Epiphany Branch Library and the central branch of the Queensboro Public Library for their aid in researching material. Finally—with much love—I want to acknowledge the contribution of my wife, Harriet Gottfried, who—as always—read and critiqued my work.

Their help was invaluable, but any shortcomings in the work are mine alone.

—Ted Gottfried

For Jonathan and Jeremy and their parents—
that they may look at all aspects of the issues involved—
peace and love.

contents

SHOULD DRUGS BE LEGALIZED?

an overview

This is a book about whether drugs, which are now illegal to sell, possess, or use, should be made legal in the United States. The controversy involves children, adolescents, and adults. It raises issues of crime and punishment, national policy, and international relations. The problem of drugs is of worldwide concern.

In June 1998, United Nations Secretary-General Kofi Annan reported that throughout the world some 21 million people "abused cocaine and heroin and 30 million abused amphetamine-type stimulants," commonly known as speed.[1] In the United States, according to a 1997–1998 survey by the Partnership for a Drug-Free America, an increasing number of children and adolescents are experimenting with drugs, particularly marijuana. A report by the National Center on Addiction and Substance Abuse at Columbia University reveals that "69 percent of federal prisoners, 76 percent of state prisoners and 70 percent of local jail inmates used drugs at least once a week before they were locked up."[2]

These statistics reflect the high cost of drugs in terms of crime and wasted human lives. Some people, however, regard drugs differently. Some question the extent of the problem. Some take issue with many of the programs designed to deal with it.

They do not all favor legalization of all drugs for all people. Most favor compromise approaches known as *decriminalization* and *harm reduction.* These terms can be confusing because different people use them to mean different things. Also, it is often hard to distinguish between legalization and decriminalization because the words are used loosely and sometimes interchangeably.

To some, decriminalization means emphasizing treatment, rather than prosecution and imprisonment, while drugs remain illegal. To others, decriminalization means a drastic reduction in the penalties for distributing, selling, or possessing drugs. To still others, it means providing free needles to addicts, financing more methadone clinics, establishing centers where addicts can take drugs legally, and other so-called harm reduction programs, which will help people use drugs more safely.

There are campaigns to legalize drugs for medical use. Programs are suggested that would make drugs legal by prescription. Others recommend that drugs be handled like liquor, with strict government supervision and penalties for selling to minors.

The National Organization for the Reform of Marijuana Laws (NORML) concentrates on the legalization of marijuana, while other groups want wider reforms, which would include heroin, cocaine, and other presently illegal substances.

A few of the reformers make claims that illegal drugs aid creativity, ease pain, and relieve tension. They point out that drug use is universal, that throughout history people have experimented with mood-altering substances, that even animals use drugs and become addicted to them. Nobody, however, is suggesting that young people should experiment with drugs.

Young bodies and minds are still developing, and drugs interfere with that development. They endanger the health of children and adolescents in a variety of ways. Drugs blur the way situations are viewed and distort judgment. The fact that drugs are illegal turns young users into criminals. And, too often, drugs can kill young people.

MARIJUANA ISSUES

Despite the dangers, the Partnership for a Drug-Free America survey found that "among children ages 9 to 12, the number who had tried marijuana rose to 571,000 last year [1997] from 334,000 in 1993." In addition, although use among 13- to 16-year-olds did not go up, "there was a significant increase among 17- and 18-year-olds to 48 percent last year from 41 percent in 1996."[3]

How many of these young people get hooked and grow up to become addicts who go on to harder drugs and criminal behavior?

This is one of the points about which those who are for and against legalization of drugs disagree. In June 1998, President Clinton proposed that the next annual federal budget contain $17 billion to fight drugs. This would include $2 billion "to extend a new advertising campaign to discourage children from using drugs."[4] But is advertising really effective in lowering drug use among young people?

Other questions have to do with adult use. Is marijuana addictive? Is it a "gateway drug" that leads to the use of more dangerous substances? Putting aside the matter of legalizing more dangerous drugs, should marijuana be made legal? Should such legalization be for medical use only? Is it right for the federal government to strike down state laws lifting restrictions on growing and using marijuana?

WHAT IS ADDICTION?

What about other drugs like cocaine, heroin, amphetamines, and crack? Does their use always lead to addiction? Is it really possible to have what is known as a maintenance habit, in

Opponents of drug legalization argue that a seemingly "harmless" drug like marijuana can act as a "gateway drug" that leads to the use of more dangerous and addicting substances such as cocaine and heroin. They fear that making marijuana legal will only serve to increase addiction, especially among young people.

which the amount and frequency of drug use are never increased? What about so-called recreational users who claim to use drugs moderately without their lives or their jobs being affected?

Is there a large drug-using population that is rarely caught, prosecuted, or imprisoned? Why are poor people who use drugs called addicts, while well-off drug users are looked at as "weekend swingers"? Do poor crack users go to jail while white-collar cocaine snorters continue partying? Is prosecution selective? Are penalties for drug use too high?

Just what is addiction, anyway? Is it a crime or an illness? Are drug addicts criminals, or are they sick people? Is addiction caused by weak will and wrong choices, or is it a reaction to the drugs themselves? What about psychological factors and chemical influences? Do genes make one person more likely to become addicted than another?

SMUGGLERS AND THE MILITARY

Some who favor legalization are concerned with the cost of stopping the flow of drugs, and with the effect our efforts are having on our relations with other countries. For example, on December 11, 1997, President Clinton announced an increase in "antidrug financing in the Defense Department's budget by $73 million to about $873 million." This money would be spent on interdiction—the program in which the military forces of the United States take action to stop the smuggling of drugs into the country. It would be used to buy "giant X-ray machines...to detect caches of cocaine hidden inside some of the 3.5 million trucks crossing into the United States at 39 entry points along the Mexican border" according to "Drug Czar" General Barry R. McCaffrey, director of the Office of National Drug Control Policy.[5]

But does interdiction really work? In the year that ended on September 30, 1997, "the Coast Guard seized 51.8 tons of cocaine, three times more than last year, and its highest total ever."[6] Impressive as that is, such records are constantly being

Federal agents unload more than 2.5 tons of cocaine in a 1989 seizure in Florida. At that time, it ranked as the seventh-largest seizure ever, but it now seems miniscule in comparison with many of the seizures that have occurred since. Even so, those who would reform drug laws ask if these seizures really result in a meaningful decrease in the supply of illegal drugs in our country.

broken. But do they really result in a meaningful decrease in drugs on the streets of our cities? And are interdiction operations hurting U.S. relations with other countries—particularly Mexico?

The United States spends "$50 billion per year in federal and state budgets" combined to fight the spread of illegal drugs.[7] Should that money be spent on military operations to stop the flow of drugs into this country from abroad? Should it be spent to arrest drug lords and drug peddlers in the United States? Should the money go for more prisons, or more treatment centers for drug addicts?

Should it be used to provide maintenance drugs to wean users away from their addictions? Should addicts be given free hypodermic needles to keep them from spreading AIDS and other diseases? Should those who are hooked on heroin be given methadone? Is methadone a cure for heroin use, or merely a substitute addiction?

Each question leads to more questions, and still more questions. The answers are hard to come by. They are always debatable. That debate involves experts with a variety of strongly held opinions. You will read about them and their views in the chapters that follow.

what drugs are; what drugs do

Yes?

No?

Maybe?

Any discussion of legalizing drugs should begin with defining them. All drugs affect the body, the mind, or both. This includes drugs prescribed by doctors, those sold over the counter without prescriptions, and those sold illegally. It may also include products not usually considered drugs, such as coffee (which contains caffeine) and tobacco (which contains nicotine).

Some drugs help people. They reduce pain. They ease mental stress. They relieve the symptoms of many illnesses. Sometimes they even cure diseases. There are also claims made for the benefits of illegal drugs. Some of them are true; some are not. They always have to be weighed against the harmful effects. There is disagreement among experts as to just how harmful these effects are. Following is a list of drugs, along with some of the facts known about them.

MARIJUANA AND HASHISH

The flowering tops and leaves of the hemp plant (*Cannabis sativa*) are the source of marijuana. Hashish is made from a dried sap that seeps from the flower tips of the plant. Mari-

*A marijuana (*Cannabis sativa) *plant*

juana looks like strands of tobacco, while hashish takes the form of a dark brown resin. Their effects are similar, but hashish is more potent.

Both affect the heart, arteries, and central nervous system to some extent. They make the user sleepy and relaxed, and they distort reality. Side effects can include memory loss, a loss of balance, and an altered sense of time. Reaction time is slowed, and this makes driving a car dangerous. There may be a long-term harmful effect on the lungs.

Marijuana has been effective in treating glaucoma, a condition resulting from a pressure in the eyes, which the drug eases. It relieves the nausea and vomiting of cancer patients undergoing chemotherapy. It also helps AIDS victims who are suffering from the effects of the treatment they receive.

COCAINE AND CRACK

For centuries, natives in the mountains of Peru have chewed the leaves of the coca bush to combat high-altitude fatigue. When the leaves are made into a paste and dried, the result is cocaine, a powder, which when sniffed is absorbed into the body. The paste can also be chemically treated to produce pure crystals of crack. The process is called freebasing. It involves boiling the crystals in solutions of sugar, or baking soda, alcohol, ether, or even baby laxatives. The term freebasing also refers to a method of smoking crack cocaine.

Cocaine increases the heart rate and decreases the appetite. It brings on a high and sometimes improves mental and physical capacity. The effects last for roughly two hours, depending on how it is used. After that, convulsions may occur. The long-term sniffing of cocaine breaks down the cartilage of the nose, causing the nose itself to have a puttylike appearance.

Crack cocaine is usually sold on the streets of poor neighborhoods. Because there is little quality control of street sales, impurities are usual and bad experiences are common. Some lead to death.

HEROIN

Opium poppies are flowers grown in many Asian countries. When they blossom, the pods are cut to release a milky juice. Exposed to the air, the juice turns brown and hardens. The resulting lumps are raw opium. When these are powdered—and usually diluted—heroin is the result.

Cocaine is a powder made from the leaves of the coca bush. It is usually inhaled.

The drug's effect can depend on just how much it is cut with other substances. The pure opium smoked in the water pipes of opium dens often results in stupors, which last for days. This is not as potentially lethal, however, as heroin—even thinned-out heroin—is when it is injected.

Injecting heroin into a vein is called mainlining. Heroin can also be sniffed, smoked, or swallowed, but it is most effective when introduced directly into the bloodstream with a needle. Then pain vanishes, cares disappear, and time stops.

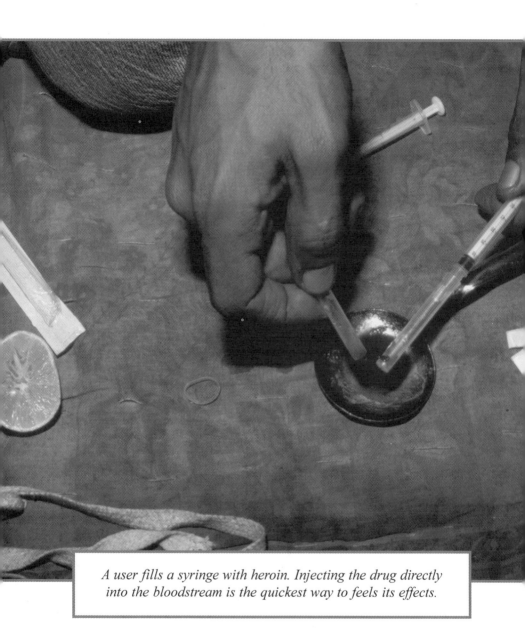

A user fills a syringe with heroin. Injecting the drug directly into the bloodstream is the quickest way to feels its effects.

The initial high is a feeling of extreme relief. It is hard to say at which point this becomes the numbness and lethargy of a trance.

Many users overdose and die because they have misjudged the potency of the heroin they have bought and overestimated how much to inject. Their respiratory systems are depressed, they can't get enough air into their lungs, and they can choke to death. Another common danger has to do with the needles used. Repeated use damages veins, and blood poisoning is a risk. Infections are common. Because addicts often share needles, hepatitis and HIV (the AIDS virus) are spread. AIDS is further spread to those who have sex with addicts.

When the effects wear off, the heroin user suffers severe depression. More heroin is the only way to get over it. This helps to make heroin extremely addictive. The addict experiences the full weight of a "monkey on his back."

If the addict tries to kick the heroin habit, withdrawal symptoms—chills, aches, insomnia, and nausea—begin within four to six hours. They intensify over the next ten to twenty hours. Within two to three days vomiting, stomach cramps, and severe tremors make the experience intolerable. This can go on for more than a week during which there is severe weight loss. Nevertheless, some people argue that heroin withdrawal is no worse than the flu.

The synthetic drug methadone is most often used to break the heroin habit. It has a similar effect to heroin, but can be taken by mouth, and its effects last much longer. It does not produce a heroin-type high, and has fewer adverse health effects. Once substituted for heroin, the methadone doses are gradually reduced until the patient is no longer dependent on them. Some doctors believe that this treatment turns heroin addicts into methadone addicts without really helping them. Even so, the quality of methadone is controlled by medical authorities, while the heroin buyer can never be sure of either the strength of the heroin or its impurities.

HALLUCINOGENS

LSD, Angel Dust (also known as PCP), mescaline (found in the peyote cactus), psilocybin (found in certain mushrooms), and Ecstasy are all hallucinogens. They are mind-altering drugs. The user experiences a so-called trip in which reality is distorted. Those who praise these drugs call them "psychedelics, on the notion that they reveal the mind."[1]

Hallucinogens are fast acting, and the physical effects are uncomfortable. Dizziness, weakness, shaking, a tingling of the skin, and nausea may be experienced all at the same time, or following one another. The nervous system is stimulated and becomes overactive.

Other short-term effects include dilated pupils and blurring of vision, increased blood pressure and heart rate, dulled hearing, mood changes, loss of concentration, and an altered sense of time. The most prominent short-term effect is the trip itself—the hallucination. How long that lasts depends on the dose, but it is usually measured in hours.

Because it is hard to know just how much to take, bad trips are common. The user "crashes" and experiences a panic reaction, which can last a long time. "Acute psychoses or depressive reactions" occur. "Errors of judgment may lead to reckless acts that threaten the user's life."[2]

Angel Dust (PCP) is the hallucinogen with the worst street reputation. This is because of the difficulty of measuring its strength and predicting its effects. There have been accidents and even deaths from behavior inflamed by overdoses.

Ecstasy is a so-called designer drug, created by chemists with ingredients that vary from one batch to the next. It has been called a love drug . . . which can heighten sexual performance, but there is no evidence to back that up. Swallowed as a pill or capsule, it acts on the user like LSD. In larger doses, however, the effects are more like the amphetamine drugs known as speed. Ecstasy is perhaps the most unstable and unpredictable of the hallucinogens.

Various claims have been made in support of hallucinogens. LSD has been touted as a cure for alcoholism. Mescaline and LSD both have been experimented with as an aid to psychotherapy. It has been suggested that the use of hallucinogens by cancer patients may ease pain and reduce the need for opiates.

SPEED

Speed, also known as uppers, refers to a group of synthetic drugs called amphetamines. They chemically resemble ephedrine, a mild stimulant, which is used to relieve asthma. Ephedrine is not as strong as some other amphetamines used to unstuff noses, fight sleepiness, increase alertness, and promote weight loss.

Abuse of amphetamines began with people taking pills to stay awake or for energy. Dexedrine, Dexamill, No-Doz, and other forms of prescription and over-the-counter speed drugs were gobbled in tablet form by people as a way of maintaining a high energy level and increasing their powers of concentration. Overweight people popped the pills to suppress their appetites. College students used uppers to stay awake while cramming for exams.

Today illegal speed appears in other forms. Drug dealers package it under a variety of names and sometimes mix it with other drugs, selling it as a powder or a liquid. It is usually sniffed like cocaine, sometimes smoked, and often—more dangerously—injected.

The effects last for several hours, but when they wear off the most moderate user will experience depression and hunger. When those who use speed intravenously crash, they are very weary, ravenously hungry, and may become paranoid. Used over a period of time, amphetamines may cause permanent psychological damage.

CAFFEINE

Caffeine stands out as a legal amphetamine. It is an ingredient of coffee, tea, cocoa, and many soft drinks. Heavy caffeine drinkers "often become nervous, irritable, apprehensive, restless, and unable to sleep."[3] They risk "respiratory ailment, possible bone loss, and other health worries."[4]

No matter what town or city you're in, there's a good chance that there's a coffee shop close by. That's not surprising considering that coffee contains caffeine, an addicting substance. The fact that caffeine is a legal drug does not negate its harmful effects, especially on young people.

Young people are increasingly becoming hooked on caffeine. An article in *The Nation* points out that "major caffeine suppliers to kids have been throwing millions into advertising and giveaways."[5] Caffeine is the one harmful drug than can be sold legally to young people.

On the other hand, according to a study at the University of Western Australia, the caffeine in coffee and tea prevents the "rapid drop in blood pressure" that can make older people feel faint after they eat.[6] In treatment programs for drug addiction and alcoholism, coffee is served to those being helped. Recently, however, many of these programs have banned coffee that is not decaffeinated.

STEROIDS

Unlike caffeine products, steroids, while legal, can only be administered by a doctor or bought by prescription. They are very useful in treating inflammations such as gout, Addison's disease, and arthritis.

The most commonly used steroids are derived from the male sex hormone testosterone. Since the 1950s they have been used by athletes and bodybuilders to increase strength and weight and to improve athletic performance. Many amateur and professional sports forbid the use of steroids, and athletes who use them risk being barred from competition.

Both the U.S. Food and Drug Administration and the American College of Sports Medicine say that steroids can be harmful. Nevertheless, today more and more adolescent males are using steroids to build themselves up. The short-term risks for them include acne, balding, reduced sex drive, and irritability. Young women who use steroids to increase their athletic ability can develop masculine characteristics, such as hair on their faces and bodies and deepened voices. All users may become aggressive, depressed, or develop other psychiatric disorders. Long-term effects include heart disease and liver damage.

TRANQUILIZERS

Tranquilizers are the most frequently prescribed drugs in the United States. Drugs such as Valium, Librium, Equanil, Miltown, Xanax, and others are used to relieve anxiety, tension, panic attacks, insomnia, headaches, and gastric discom-

*Ben Johnson of Canada was stripped of his 1988
Olympic gold medal in the men's 100-meter event after
he tested positive for steroids. The drugs can enhance
athletic performance, thereby giving some an unfair
advantage, and so were banned by the Olympic Committee.
But the health risks involved far outweigh
any perceived benefits of steroids.*

fort. They provide only temporary relief, however, and the effects are not long lasting.

The drugs mildly depress the central nervous system, and mask symptoms without treating causes. Patients can become dependent on them, but with continued use their effectiveness decreases.

Prolonged use of tranquilizers can lead to deep depression. Sometimes the patient stops caring and stops functioning. In combination with alcohol, these pills are particularly dangerous. Overdosing on tranquilizer pills swallowed with alcohol is a frequent means of suicide.

ALCOHOL

Alcohol, which is sold legally (but not to minors), does more damage in the United States than all the illegal drugs combined. According to the National Institute on Alcohol Abuse and Alcoholism, the cost is "an estimated $98 billion and 100,000 lives per year. . . . One-half of all traffic fatalities and one-third of all traffic injuries are related to the abuse of alcohol. Also, one-third of all suicides and one-third of all mental health disorders are estimated to be associated with serious alcohol abuse. Accidents associated with alcohol problems are especially prominent among teenagers. It has been estimated that there are over four million problem drinkers between the ages of fourteen and seventeen in the United States."[7]

In addition, 7.4 percent of adult Americans—14 million people—are alcoholics. About 75 percent are male, and 25 percent are women. One out of three families in the United States is affected by a drinking problem.

The health effects related to heavy drinking include cirrhosis of the liver, cancer of the mouth and throat, ulcers, and inflammation of the pancreas. The nervous system is affected, causing blackouts and delirium tremens (d.t.'s). Pregnant women who drink may give birth to babies with fetal alcohol syndrome, which can cause mental and physical birth defects. Binge drinking—consuming large amounts of alcoholic beverages in a short period of time—has caused brain damage and sometimes death among young people.

Alcoholics are often aggressive. Problem drinkers are the rule, rather than the exception, among wife beaters and child abusers. By lowering inhibitions, alcohol too often releases antisocial behavior.

Nevertheless, according to some medical experts, "moderate or temperate use of alcohol is not harmful."[8] In 1998 the American Heart Association concluded that "the incidence of heart disease in those who consume moderate amounts of alcohol (an average of one to two drinks per day for men and one drink per day for women) is lower than in nondrinkers."[9] Studies at Harvard and the University of Wisconsin concluded that red wine minimizes the clogging of arteries by cholesterol and may reduce the risk of coronary heart disease by as much as 40 percent. In countries like France and Italy, which "have a permissive attitude toward drinking but a negative one toward drunkenness, the proportion of alcohol users . . . is high but the rate of alcoholism is low."[10]

NICOTINE

Cigarettes, cigars, pipe tobacco, and chewing tobacco all contain nicotine. Found mostly in the tobacco leaves, it is the most potent ingredient of the plant. Tobacco is the seventh-largest crop in the United States. It is grown on 160,000 farms, all of which are financed in part by the U.S. Department of Agriculture through its price-support system.

Yet "smoking is far more lethal than drinking, claiming an estimated 400,000 lives a year to alcohol's 110,000."[11] The surgeon general of the United States has determined that tobacco can cause cancer. The American Heart Association finds that smoking is a major factor in heart disease.

The Centers for Disease Control and Prevention's 1997 survey found that "among white students, 39.7 percent said they smoked cigarettes, up from 30.9 percent six years earlier. Among Hispanic students, more than one third now say they smoke, up from roughly a quarter. Among black youths, 22.7

Despite laws prohibiting the sale of cigarettes to anyone under the age of eighteen, younger teens have no trouble buying cigarettes. Nor do most of them feel that increasing the price of cigarettes (through government measures to increase taxes on tobacco, for example) would stop them from smoking.

percent list themselves as smokers, compared with the 12.6 [percent] who said they smoked in 1991."[12]

According to an article in *The New York Times,* "the students were perfectly aware of the health hazards of cigarette smoking."[13] The question for cigarette smokers is the same as it is for all drug users. Why do people who are well aware of the dangers of drugs use them in the first place? Why do young people, and adults as well, seek out substances that are harmful to their health, and that they know can or will lead to addiction and dependency?

addiction and dependency

Yes?
No?
Maybe?

Coffee is always available in the office where Debbie works as a secretary, and she drinks four or five cups a day. Her mother takes a Valium pill every morning and another before bed. Debbie's younger sister, Wendy, occasionally smokes marijuana when she baby-sits. Wendy's boyfriend, Bruce, trips on LSD. His father regularly uses a cough medicine containing codeine, a painkiller. Bruce's boss, Mr. Allen, has one or two martinis every afternoon before going home from his high-pressure job in publishing. Mr. Allen lives next door to Debbie and Wendy, whose father smokes three packs of cigarettes a day.

Which of these seven people has an addiction? Does the substance used define any of them as an addict? Is it the frequency of use, or the length of time a drug has been taken that defines addiction? Or is it the behavior of the user after taking it?

Debbie is energized. Wendy spaces out. So does her mother. Bruce has visions and is disoriented. His father feels no pain and nods off. Mr. Allen relaxes and heads home with a pleasant buzz. Wendy's father coughs constantly, is short of breath, and has occasional chest pains. Does their behavior define them as addicts?

The World Health Organization (WHO) defines addictive drugs as those that "produce in the great majority of users an irresistible need for the drug, an increased tolerance to its effect, and a physical dependence as indicated by severe and painful symptoms when the drug is withdrawn." WHO makes a distinction between addictive drugs and habit-forming drugs, which "cause an emotional or psychological, rather than a physical, dependence in the user and . . . can be withdrawn without causing physical harm or pain." The difference between habit-forming and addictive drugs according to WHO is "the type of dependence. If the dependence is purely psychological, it can be considered a habit. If it is physical, it is an addiction."[1]

According to most experts, "marijuana is not physically addictive"—meaning that there is neither bodily craving nor dependency. "Susceptible people," however, can "develop a psychological dependence."[2] Tolerance can be built up and this may or may not lead to increased doses.

Strictly speaking, pot-smoking Wendy is not addicted because she does not have a *physical* dependence on marijuana. Nor is her mother *physically* dependent on Valium. LSD tripper Bruce and martini drinker Mr. Allen may have psychological needs, which help to make them dependent, but the substances they are using are not actually *physically* addictive.

However, the nicotine in the cigarettes Debbie's father smokes is "the most widely used addicting drug in American society" and "affects the chemistry of the brain."[3] The codeine in the cough syrup used by Bruce's father comes from the opium poppy, and if he were to stop taking it, he would experience withdrawal symptoms similar to those of morphine.

Debbie is addicted to coffee because the large amount of caffeine she takes in jazzes up her nervous and circulatory systems, allowing her to function physically in a high-powered manner that would be impaired if she gave up coffee.

To sum up, neither marijuana, tranquilizers, nor LSD are physically addictive. They may be habit-forming for some people, who form an emotional or psychological dependence on them, but they will not suffer physical pain if they give up these substances. Alcohol is not addictive for Mr. Allen, but it might be for others who cannot limit themselves to one or two drinks a day.

COCAINE DEPENDENCY

Cocaine dependency is not so easily categorized. Some doctors believe that because its effects feel so good, cocaine is highly addictive. However, an early study by the Drug Abuse Council concluded that "medical experts generally agree that cocaine produces few observable health consequences in its users."[4] Notables from psychoanalyst Sigmund Freud to author William Burroughs have praised cocaine as an aid to creativity. Critics believe that those who use it for that purpose are deluding themselves.

The effects of crack are more harmful. When smoked, it reaches the brain in a matter of seconds, and there is an instant high. Because it acts so quickly and so potently, crack is much more psychologically addictive than ordinary cocaine.

DIFFERENT FOLKS, DIFFERENT STROKES

Why does cocaine—and other drugs as well—prove addictive to some people and not to others? Why can some people have one or two drinks a day and suffer no harm, while others take a sip of wine and can't stop themselves from going off on a roaring binge? Why can some people sample marijuana and go no further, while others get hooked?

Science offers a variety of answers. They begin with the fact that each person is physically and psychologically different from every other person. As the saying goes, it's in the genes. Some of us are born with allergies passed down from our parents, or perhaps from their parents. Some of us are born

Dr. Sigmund Freud, who founded psychoanalysis in the late 1800s, touted cocaine as an aid to creativity. It is doubtful that Freud was aware of the extent of cocaine's addictiveness.

with traits that make us violently ill when we drink or smoke marijuana. Some of us are born with a built-in compulsion that won't let us stop once we drink or take drugs. We are said to have a "genetic predisposition," or an "addictive personality."

Of course it's not that simple. There are people who develop a dependency on drugs over a period of time. The drugs cause chemical changes in the body or the brain. The user's metabolism changes. A dependency is created.

CAN "JUST SAY NO!" WORK?

There is a difference between dependency and addiction and habits, which are difficult to break. So-called behavioral addictions like gambling, overeating, compulsive sex, and others are not really addictions at all. They are habit patterns. They are the result of deep-seated psychological pressures.

This does not mean that they are easy to overcome. Marijuana, for instance, may not be addictive, but that does not mean that the marijuana habit is easy to kick. It takes willpower. But willpower depends on the individual, the circumstances, the setting, the timing, emotions, and a number of other factors.

Just say no!—the slogan originated by First Lady Nancy Reagan for the antidrug campaign targeting children, which she headed—is good advice when it comes to drugs. However, many of those who counsel substance abusers feel that it fails to deal with the underlying causes of drug use. Those three words too often can't overcome the peer pressure put on first-time users. They are even less effective with those who have already gotten into drugs.

BIRDS, BEASTS, AND BERRIES

The question came up at the end of the last chapter. Now we ask it again: Why do people use drugs? The answer may be that humans are part of the animal kingdom. According to psychopharmacologist and World Health Organization consultant Dr. Ronald K. Siegel, "almost every species of animals has engaged in the natural pursuit of intoxicants."[5]

It would seem to be an instinct, as well as a habit pattern. For instance, every February thousands of robins descend on the small town of Pleasant Hills, California. They head straight for groves of trees laden with ripening toyon berries. These berries contain an unidentified hallucinogen. The birds gorge themselves on the berries and get high. They smash themselves against closed windows and dive into speeding cars. Others wobble around on the ground, too drugged to fly. The binge lasts for three weeks with the birds returning day after day to strip the toyon berries from the trees. In the neighboring town of Walnut Creek, a "drunk tank" has been set up where stoned birds are held until the effects of the berries wear off.

The birds' behavior is like that of elephants in Asia and Africa in districts where rice or fruit grows abundantly and often rots and ferments. These fermented substances make the elephants intoxicated. Herds will travel as far as 20 miles (32 kilometers) a day to gorge themselves on fruit mash or rice mash. Following such sprees, the elephants sometimes become violent. In West Bengal, India, a herd 150 strong broke into a compound where rice mash was stored. The stampede destroyed seven concrete buildings and killed five people.

ANIMAL ADDICTS

Dr. Siegel writes that "whenever seed-eating birds have been given the opportunity to feast on marijuana seeds, they have done so with relish." Their "love for marijuana seeds," he points out, "has endured for thousands of years."[6] Nor are they the only nonhuman, pot-loving creatures.

In the basements of police stations where seized marijuana is stored, the bags are often broken into by mice and rats, which feast on the contents. In marijuana fields in Hawaii, cows and horses feed on the flowers of the plants and stagger around. In European fields, lambs become "gay and crazy."[7] Dr. Siegel observed grasshoppers "executing unusual jumps from the marijuana leaves" of plants in a field in the Midwest.[8]

He also notes that "opium fields are favorite hunting grounds for a variety of insects, birds and rodents."[9]

NOBODY LIVES FOREVER

Nobody really knows why insects, animals, and humans seek out intoxicating substances. One theory put forth by some psychologists is that it has to do with death. All creatures know from observation that they are eventually going to die. This knowledge also comes from instinct.

Death is not a happy prospect for many people. Drugs and alcohol can temporarily ease the burden of their knowledge of death, blur it, and give the illusion of pushing death away. Unable to face the reality, people seek refuge from it in the unreality of drugs.

That is one theory. It may or may not be true. However, while drugs or alcohol may help us forget our mortality for a while, they can't prevent death. The important thing to remember is that too often they can cause death.

chapter four

Yes? No?
human weakness
or human nature?
Maybe?

Human beings have always used, and often abused mind-altering substances. In biblical times, according to Genesis, Noah "drank of the wine, and was drunken."[1] Sumerian records dating from 5000 B.C. mention use of the fruit of the poppy, which we know as opium. In 400 B.C. Hippocrates, the father of modern medicine, prescribed opium to an extent we now know to be addictive. In the eleventh century, hashish, named after the founder of the Society of Assassins, was widely used in Persia.

Hallucinogens such as "sacred" mushrooms and the juice of the peyote cactus were used by the Aztecs and the Maya two thousand years ago. Tobacco leaves containing nicotine were regularly chewed and smoked by the North American natives who introduced the practice to European explorers and settlers. In exchange, the Europeans gave the Native Americans various fermented beverages capable of making them as drunk as Noah.

THE OPIUM WAR

As smoking and chewing tobacco became popular in Europe, the tobacco trade flourished and became highly profitable in the Netherlands and England. By the 1700s, however, commerce in opium was becoming even more profitable. The poppy flowers were grown in India, and the opium distilled from them was exported to China in awesome quantities. It was as if the entire Chinese nation, the most populous in the world, was becoming hooked on the drug.

The British East India Company had an official monopoly over the import of drugs into China. When the Manchus, who ruled the country in the early 1800s, first tried to stop the opium trade because of the violence it engendered, they were unsuccessful. It took many years before the monopoly was finally broken. When it was, however, that did not stop the flow of opium into China. On the contrary, it encouraged competition, and soon the country was flooded with low-priced opium.

United States and French companies now competed with the British to ship opium to China. The Manchu government put its foot down. It ordered all foreign merchants to surrender their stocks of opium so that they might be destroyed. The British refused, and the Opium War broke out, raging from 1839 through 1842. The Chinese were defeated and were forced into a series of treaties with Britain, France, the United States, and other countries, which reestablished the opium trade, although it remained illegal under Chinese law.

In 1858 the Treaty of Tientsin legalized the importation of opium into China. A tariff on the drug allowed the Chinese government to share in the profits. As a result, an illegal opium trade developed with the purpose of avoiding the tariff. Gangs of smugglers formed themselves into secret societies, which expanded their activities to piracy, hijacking, and other forms of gangsterism.

WHISKEY, COCAINE, AND ABRAHAM LINCOLN

During this period, Abraham Lincoln was elected president of the United States, and the Civil War broke out. According to historian Henry Pratt, shortly before Lincoln's election, on October 12, 1860, he "walked into the drugstore and purchased a bottle of cocaine for fifty cents."[2] It was not to be snorted or swallowed, but rather to be used as a hair tonic to help in the growing of Lincoln's new beard.

Cocaine was only one of a variety of names under which coca products were openly sold at that time. They were not yet regarded as harmful and were present in many patent medicines and cooking extracts. Opium was also present in many candies and other over-the-counter products.

The drug that most concerned Americans at this time was neither opium nor cocaine, but alcohol. In relation to alcohol, Abraham Lincoln is remembered for his reply to a temperance committee who wanted him to dismiss General Ulysses S. Grant, the victor of the Battle of Vicksburg, because of his heavy drinking. Lincoln asked the committee what brand of whiskey Grant drank, adding that he wanted to send a case of it to each of his other generals.

Nevertheless, Lincoln recognized the problem posed by drinking and regarded it as "a universal appetite for intoxication." He thought that "the practice of drinking . . . is just as old as the world itself." He believed that those who "have never fallen victims [to liquor] have been spared more by the absence of appetite than from any mental or moral superiority over those who have."[3]

Smoking went hand in hand with drinking during this period. Cigarettes—as distinguished from chewing tobacco, pipe tobacco, and the occasional cigar—were becoming increasingly popular. In 1855 the safety match was invented. It reduced the chance among those who both smoked and drank of setting fire to themselves while under the influence of alcohol. The Diamond Match Company manufactured a "Drunkard's Match," which put itself out automatically when it burned halfway down.

WOMEN AND CHILDREN FIRST

A case might be made that in the mid-nineteenth century more harm was done by the medical profession than by whiskey distillers or tobacco sellers. British doctors were impressed by evidence from India of the soothing effects on colicky infants of milk and poppy seed drinks. The preparation was—and is—harmless. However, in England, and later in the United States, the drink was altered to become a laudanum syrup containing opium, which is the juice of the poppy, rather than the harmless seed. According to WHO consultant Dr. Siegel, "these 'quieting' syrups were helpful to mothers and baby-sitters alike, but . . . hundreds of infants died; thousands suffered addiction and withdrawal."[4]

In the United States, as in England, opiates were regarded as cure-alls and were freely prescribed by doctors for adults as well as children. Prescriptions, however, were not really needed. Addiction to over-the-counter opiates skyrocketed, with laudanum leading the way. It was widely used by women to relieve the discomfort of their menstrual cycles. There was a particularly "high addiction rate among women (three times the rate among men)."[5]

The Civil War changed that. About twenty years before, the hypodermic needle had been invented. It was widely used to inject morphine, a form of opium, to relieve the pain of wounded soldiers. Army doctors regarded morphine as a miracle drug.

They were not unaware of its potential for addiction. However, they mistakenly thought that if the drug was administered in a way that kept it from reaching the stomach, no addiction would develop. As a result of this belief, they injected the morphine directly into the veins of their patients. They were, in effect, mainlining the drug. The practice "produced large numbers of addicted soldiers (about 400,000 during the Civil War)."[6]

AMERICAN OPIUM DENS

After the Civil War, the companies building the railroads, which would crisscross America, went to China to solicit cheap labor to clear obstacles and lay track. Hundreds of thousands of Chinese were drawn to the United States by exaggerated promises of jobs and unlimited opportunities. What they

> At the top of this page of advertisements from the 1880s is a pitch for "A Reliable Wine of Coca." Drinking this wine, which contained what we know as cocaine, was said to result in "a general feeling of pleasantness." It seems ironic that some were already concerned by the harmful effects of opium addiction, as evidenced by the ad further down the page for a cure for this addiction.

found was indentured servitude, which kept them indebted to the railroad companies for the cost of their room and board. Their only solace was the water pipes they brought with them from China and the opium they smoked in them.

Opium dens sprang up along the railroads' right of way and in cities with large Chinese populations like San Francisco and New York. Soon their customers were not limited to Chinese Americans. Partying whites visited them, and some returned again and again to become opium addicts.

As competition to sell opium grew, there were so-called Tong Wars among distributors' gangs, and the federal government became alarmed. A series of laws were passed. These included import taxes on opium, penalties against smoking it, and the closing of opium dens. The main effect of these laws was to drive the opium users underground. The smoking of opium continued to grow.

THE PAUSE THAT REFRESHES

At the same time, patent medicines containing opium and cocaine were legal and easily available. Pure cocaine was sold legally over the counter. Both substances were used legally in food products.

In 1886, John Pemberton of Atlanta, Georgia, devised the formula for the soft drink that the world would come to know as Coca-Cola. It was made from the cola nut and small quantities of the coca leaf. This is, of course, the leaf from which cocaine is derived.

A bottle of Coca-Cola sold for a nickel. Each 8-ounce (227-gram) bottle contained .0021 ounce (60 milligrams) of cocaine. The soft drink's slogan was "the pause that refreshes." Coca-Cola was an overwhelming hit with the soda-drinking public.

Over the next twenty years more than seventy brands of soda pop containing cocaine appeared on the market to compete with Coca-Cola. But Coke remained by far the leading brand, and growing numbers of people were becoming addicted to it. Dr. Siegel writes that "some southerners were consuming fifty bottles a day of Coca-Cola in order to get more of the cocaine."[7]

Legislators became alarmed by the health risks posed by such consumption. There was talk of passing laws against soft drinks containing cocaine. Before that happened, in 1903, Coca-Cola removed the cocaine from its product. Other beverage manufacturers switched from cocaine to caffeine.

THE HAGUE CONVENTION

Three years later, in 1906, Congress passed the Pure Food and Drug Act. This required that all the ingredients of a product be listed on the package label. It did not prohibit the use of cocaine and opium in food and drugs. It only said they had to be identified among the ingredients. Such listings were usually in very small type and were not really effective in alerting the consumer to the presence of the dangerous substances.

Three more years went by before legislation banning the importation and possession of opium was passed. The immediate result was smuggling, which grew into a major illegal business. The price of opium skyrocketed. The profit margin between growers, middlemen, and sellers multiplied. Many addicts switched over to morphine and heroin, opiates that were diluted, cheaper, and more readily available.

Opium was a problem that concerned President Theodore Roosevelt on an international level. The gangsterism spawned by opium in China was spreading to other countries. Roosevelt called a meeting of thirteen nations in Shanghai to deal with the problems of the Chinese opium trade. The recommendations of that meeting were taken to the first international opium convention in The Hague in 1912. Worldwide regulation of opium was ratified by The Hague Convention in 1913 and 1914. However, when World War I broke out, drug problems were put on hold. It was not until 1920 that the League of Nations took over the responsibility "to supervise agreements with regard to the traffic in opium and other dangerous drugs."[8]

During the early 1900s there was growing concern among Americans regarding the use of drugs and alcohol. In 1914 the Harrison Narcotics Act was enacted into law by Congress. It did not ban drugs outright. Rather it was "a law for the orderly marketing of these drugs in small quantities over the counter and in larger quantities on a physician's prescription."[9]

The law did not cover marijuana, tobacco products, caffeine, or alcohol. Strong lobbying by the pharmaceutical industry had protected marijuana. The tobacco industry had seen to it that its products were not covered. The fact was that many legislators smoked, and many kept snuff boxes on their desks, which might contain tobacco, marijuana, or even occasionally cocaine.

Nevertheless, the Harrison Act did succeed in putting a stop to the sale of most over-the-counter narcotics. The result was the establishment of black markets in cities across the nation. Districts devoted to gambling and prostitution now became areas where opium and cocaine were available. Soon the underground traffic linked up with international smugglers. The drugs flowed freely, but not much attention was paid because America was now focused on a different intoxicating product.

CARRY NATION
TOOK AN AX...

On June 5, 1900, a 6-foot (2-meter) tall, 175-pound (79-kilogram) woman armed with stones and bricks entered a saloon in Kiowa, Kansas, and made an announcement: "Men, I have come to save you from a drunkard's fate!" She then proceeded to smash every bottle in the place, bashed in kegs of beer with a hatchet, and wrecked the mirror behind the bar and the saloon's front window. Afterward she "went through Kiowa like a tornado, destroying six saloons."[10]

Carry Nation may have gone down in history as something of a larger-than-life teetotaling folk icon, but the ills she acted out against were very real. Alcohol addiction was taking its toll on families, and does to this day.

Her name was Carry A. Nation. She was fifty-three years old, and her first husband had died of alcoholism after two years of marriage. Her one-woman campaign against demon rum soon attracted followers, hymn-singing women who had suffered the beatings of drunken husbands and the poverty of food money spent in saloons. They were the core of a temperance movement, which would one day result in the passing of Prohibition, the Eighteenth Amendment to the Constitution, which forbade the selling and drinking of liquor in the United States.

Carry Nation was not punished for wrecking the barrooms of Kansas with her hatchet and bricks. Kansas was a "dry" state, which meant that liquor was illegal within its borders. As the temperance movement grew, other states became dry as well. The Anti-Saloon League was founded in 1906, and by the time Prohibition went into effect on October 28, 1919, thirty-three states containing 63 percent of the population of the United States were already dry.

PROHIBITION

The 1920s were the Jazz Age, the time of flappers, the Charleston, and illegal drinking establishments called speakeasies. There were 200,000 of these speakeasies across the country. In New York City alone, Prohibition did away with 15,000 saloons. They were replaced by 32,000 speakeasies. These speakeasies, with the slots in their front doors, muscle-bound guardians, and secret passwords were supplied by giant bootlegging organizations run by criminal gangs across the country.

Prohibition had given birth to a crime wave. There were turf battles among gangs, hijacking of trucks and piracy of smugglers' boats, and widespread killings with the rattle of tommy guns bringing death to innocent pedestrians as well as gangland targets. There was also widespread corruption among those charged with enforcing the new law.

Between 1920 and 1928 the Treasury Department fired 706 agents and prosecuted another 257 for taking bribes. In

New York City, Police Captain Daniel Chapin lined up his speakeasy squad and announced that "everyone...with a diamond ring is fired."[11] Half the squad had to go.

It didn't take long for even the nondrinking public to become disenchanted with Prohibition. It was common knowledge that U.S. President Warren Harding drank whiskey and beer in the privacy of the White House. More and more people were going to speakeasies. More and more solitary drinkers were dying from the effects of illegal, poorly produced whiskey. Finally, in 1933, the Twenty-first Amendment was passed and Prohibition was repealed. By 1966 there were no more dry states.

TEA PADS AND POT PATCHES

Now, slowly, the attention of the country turned from liquor to marijuana. Prohibition had seen an increase in the black marketing of the drug. Parlors where marijuana was smoked, called "tea pads . . . started to appear in New Orleans and other southern cities that were the port of entry for marijuana smuggled from Cuba and Mexico."[12] By 1930, New York City had five hundred tea pads where marijuana smokers gathered.

Individual states began to pass laws against marijuana. By 1937, forty-six states had outlawed it. That same year Congress passed the Marihuana [sic] Tax Act. It required registration with the government and payment of a tax by anyone dealing in marijuana. It made it hard for people to purchase marijuana for nonmedical use.

Despite a Federal Bureau of Narcotics campaign portraying it as a violent menace, marijuana use did not fall off. Tea pads moved into the former speakeasies. Users began planting hemp patches and growing their own marijuana in rural areas around the country.

Most of the marijuana, however, still came from Mexico. In 1945 seizures of the substance became a top priority for U.S. border patrols. In that year more marijuana was confiscated on the border than was seized in the entire United States.

An increase in crime and widespread corruption made many people think twice about the logic of Prohibition. Those who wanted to drink found ways to do so, even if it meant concealing a flask in one's boot.

VIETNAM AND DRUGS

Throughout the late 1940s and 1950s, marijuana was a problem that was associated in the public mind mostly with musicians. The image of crazed, reefer-smoking jazz drummers was common. But marijuana hadn't really gone away. It had only gone underground.

It was widely used by American troops in Vietnam. It was so common that the army "began an all-out campaign to cut off the supply—with pot-sniffing dogs, searches of men's billets, and mass arrests for possession." Two years after the campaign was launched, a Pentagon researcher went to Vietnam to study its effectiveness. He found that many soldiers had stopped smoking marijuana and started using "heroin, which was odorless, far less bulky than pot, and in Vietnam, extremely inexpensive."[13]

Meanwhile, young people were smoking marijuana openly on the streets of America. Parents were frantic. The country's leaders had to be concerned. The result of that concern was the declaration of the War on Drugs.

the war on drugs

Yes? No?

Maybe?

Two months before the 1968 presidential election, Republican candidate Richard M. Nixon fired the opening salvo of the War on Drugs. In a speech to a rally at Disneyland, Nixon singled out "the problem of narcotics" as "the modern curse of the youth" of the country. He blamed an increase in crime on drug addicts. He promised to "accelerate the development of tools and weapons" needed to fight the plague of drugs.[1]

Nixon was zeroing in on a national concern. *Newsweek* had reported that "the age of U.S. drug users is dropping rapidly." *Life* had confirmed the pictures on the television nightly news. "Drug abuse and marijuana," the magazine reported, "are now very much in the open."[2]

Now identified with young antiwar protesters, marijuana was the country's most widely used illegal drug. There were roughly one hundred pot smokers for every heroin user. As for legal drugs, a 1967 U.S. government report showed that "sales of sedatives and tranquilizers had increased 535 percent between 1953 and 1965."[3] However, it was "grass" (as marijuana was popularly known), which was believed to be fueling the rebellion on college campuses and the race riots in the nation's ghettos.

The signs in the image read:

The Poverty of our Foreign Policy is Causing War

END THE DRAFT— LET YOUNG MEN LIVE

STOP THE WAR NOW!

I AM NOT A COMMUNIST AND I STILL OPPOSE THE WAR IN VIETNAM

THE PEOPLE OF TH... ...ITED STATES WOU... ...OK OVER THEIR ...TIONALISTIC, REAC... ...ONARY PRIDE, THE ...AR WOULD BE OVER ...E CAN BE WRONG

Part of the youth rebellion against the Vietnam War was pot smoking. It was a symbol of defiance against the Establishment. Almost overnight, it seemed America was faced with a drug problem affecting its youth. This demonstration took place in New York City in 1967.

Following the assassinations of Reverend Martin Luther King Jr., and Senator Robert Kennedy in early 1968, a crime bill was rushed through Congress, which would increase police power in the future War on Drugs. It legitimized wiretaps and created the Law Enforcement Assistance Administration to provide federal money to local police departments. Although the bill was aimed at dealing with the rise in crime, street violence, and riots, drugs would eventually become its main target.

A year later some 400,000 young people gathered on the muddy fields of a dairy farm near Woodstock, New York, for a multistar rock and folk music concert with Vietnam War protest overtones. Shelter was inadequate, conditions were bad, and the air was thick with marijuana smoke. One doctor at the site reported an "abundance [of] bad LSD trips."[4] Nudity and other outlandish behavior associated with drugs provoked public outrage.

There followed a series of tragedies caused by drugs. One of the most publicized was the death of TV host Art Linkletter's young daughter, Diane. She killed herself during an LSD trip. "Diane was not a hippie. She was not a drug addict," Linkletter said. Drugs had killed Diane. President Richard Nixon said the tragedy "gives a lie to the idea that this is something that simply happens to the poor."[5] In 1970 rock star Jimi Hendrix and top vocalist Janis Joplin both died of drug overdoses.

A HODGEPODGE
OF PROGRAMS

That year also saw a change in the antidrug program of the federal government. The authority to rank drugs according to how dangerous they might be was taken away from the surgeon general and health officials and turned over to the narcotics division of the attorney general's office. Drugs were no longer a health problem. They were now a crime problem.

At this time there was a hodgepodge of programs to deal with drug addicts. In New York and California they were locked up in hospitals until their addiction was under control. The federal government imprisoned them in a hospital in Lexington, Kentucky. Private treatment programs like Synanon in California and Daytop Village in New York established communal living centers where addicts gave each other support while kicking their habits.

Methadone began to be widely used as a legal alternative to heroin. Addicts were given it under supervision in clinics around the country. Congress provided $7.5 million for 20 methadone centers treating 2,500 addicts.

THE NATION'S NUMBER-ONE PROBLEM

Most of the early programs were concerned with heroin, which was the least-used hard drug in America at that time. However, the idea of marijuana as a gateway drug leading to the use of more dangerous substances was becoming accepted. Nevertheless, 1970 saw the formation of the National Organization for the Reform of Marijuana Laws (NORML), which campaigned to decriminalize marijuana.

In 1971 the director of the National Institute of Mental Health said that he thought marijuana offenders should receive light punishment. President Nixon fired him. Later that year a new Detroit police commissioner went on a whirlwind campaign against heroin, closing 300 so-called shooting galleries and arresting 1,600 people. Immediately a turf war broke out among heroin dealers, and forty people died violent deaths.

The federal government tackled the problem at the source. Much of the opium smuggled into the United States came from Turkey. The United States gave Turkey $35 million in aid to destroy its opium crop. Nobody blinked at the amount. In July 1971 a poll showed that the American people considered drugs—not Vietnam, crime, or racial upheavals—to be the nation's number-one problem.

In 1973 the New York State legislature passed the Rockefeller Drug Laws. Originally proposed by Governor Nelson Rockefeller, they called for a sentence of up to fifteen years for possession of an ounce of marijuana. Life in prison was the punishment for having less than an ounce of heroin. Plea bargaining, in which a defendant agrees to plead guilty to a lesser charge, was forbidden in many drug crime cases. Thirty-one new state courts were created to handle drug cases. A national poll revealed that 66 percent of Americans favored the Rockefeller Drug Laws.

Meanwhile, Congress had combined several federal agencies into the Drug Enforcement Administration (DEA), an arm of the Justice Department. It would have the authority to prosecute illicit drug traffickers at the highest levels. Initially the DEA was not very active. The Watergate scandal and the resignation of President Nixon had pushed drugs out of the public's mind. During 1974 and 1975 the media covered only a handful of drug-related stories. Even so, the 1974 federal budget for the War on Drugs was $719 million, up from $69 million in 1969.

By 1976 and 1977 attitudes toward drugs were shifting. A man named Bob Randall was acquitted of growing marijuana on the grounds of medical necessity, and the Department of Health, Education and Welfare (HEW) provided him with three hundred marijuana cigarettes to smoke in order to relieve his glaucoma. A drug policy staff under President Gerald Ford concluded that it was unrealistic to expect to eliminate drug abuse from our society. In March 1977, in a speech to Congress, Representative Dan Quayle—one day to be vice president of the United States—recommended decriminalizing possession of marijuana.

CRACK: A WARNING!

Congress passed a law in 1978 that allowed the DEA to seize the money and property of suspected drug dealers. At this time cocaine was reemerging as the recreational drug of choice for the so-called beautiful people who sniffed it in fashionable discos and at weekend parties at wealthy homes.

The snorting of cocaine was the subject of an article in *Science* magazine in December 1979. Its author, psychiatrist Craig Van Dyke, downplayed its harm because the act of snorting slowed absorption by the brain. However, he pointed out that when cocaine is smoked there is a rush effect, which hits the brain immediately and which can have very dangerous psychological effects.

The smoking of cocaine was widespread in South America. It was just starting in the United States. The form of cocaine we know as crack was just appearing in poor neighborhoods. The crack epidemic was just beginning.

MARIJUANA IS TARGETED

In 1980 the DEA wrote a model law aimed at banning drug-related paraphernalia and circulated it to all the state legislatures. As a result, many states passed laws against the sale of such items as water pipes, syringes and needles, seeds for hemp plants, and papers for rolling cigarettes. The laws were aimed at breaking the hold of the drug culture on young people.

The following year, under orders from President Ronald Reagan, the FBI became involved in drug investigations for the first time. The agency's drug budget was increased by 50 percent. The Coast Guard received a 44 percent budget increase to fight drug smugglers.

It was decided that since marijuana was the drug most used by young people, it should be the main target of the War on Drugs. The theory of grass as a gateway drug leading to harder drugs was impressed on the public. The campaign against it was framed as a struggle against permissive parenting. Hard-rock music, torn jeans, and sexual activity were all viewed as stepping-stones leading to marijuana and from there to hard drugs.

In October 1981, *Science News* unveiled a University of Kentucky study showing marijuana to be "a cause of heroin use."[6] In 1982 a book called *Toughlove* by David and Phyllis York rocketed to the top of the best-seller lists. It advocated parents treating their marijuana-smoking children as criminals and breaking them of their habits by letting them go to jail, or holding them forcibly in treatment facilities. One such facility was run by an organization called Straight, which used such techniques as denial of privacy, sleep deprivation, the with-holding of food, and other forms of mental and physical abuse to stop its patients from using drugs.

But was marijuana addictive? In 1982 a study commissioned by the National Academy of Sciences (NAS) found that it wasn't. It also found no evidence of damage to the brain, nervous system, or fertility. However, Frank Press, the president of the NAS, disavowed the report, claiming that not enough data had been gathered to justify such a conclusion.

Meanwhile, Nancy Reagan was heavily engaged in the War on Drugs. She made speeches, gave interviews, and visited schools. On July 4, 1984, she spoke at an elementary school in Oakland, California. When a child asked her what to do if friends urged him to try grass, Mrs. Reagan had a ready answer. "Just say no!" she told him.[7] The phrase caught on immediately, and it soon became the slogan of the War on Drugs.

NEW MEASURES

The War on Drugs was heating up again. *Newsweek* reported that drugs were affecting the performance of American workers and were interfering with business productivity. A top-selling *DC Comics* series, which targeted fourth- through sixth-grade students, produced "Plague," a strip in which Teen Titans beat up drug dealers and saved a sweet-faced little girl from life as a druggie. The comic was produced "In Cooperation with the President's Drug Awareness Campaign."[8]

In the early 1980s, First Lady Nancy Reagan visited institutions run by the organization Straight and believed their programs led to recovery from drug addiction. Her involvement in the War on Drugs then contributed what would become the campaign's rallying cry: "Just say no!"

Early in 1985, Attorney General Edwin Meese III announced a new strategy. Up to now, the War on Drugs had targeted smugglers and drug dealers. In the future, Meese declared, pressure would be put on the drug user. Marijuana smokers of all ages now faced arrest and prison.

Meanwhile, crack was gaining ground in poor neighborhoods. Much of it was being smuggled in from Colombia via drug-filled balloons carried in couriers' stomachs. Customs agents confirmed this by forcing the couriers to excrete the balloons. The Supreme Court confirmed the agents' right to do this. Justice William Brennan dissented on the grounds that "government officials [cannot] require people to excrete on command."[9]

In 1986, President Reagan signed Executive Order #12564, *Drug Free Workplace*, which ordered federal agencies to test the urine of workers for evidence of drug use. First-time offenders would have to undergo counseling. Those who failed the test twice would be fired.

In Congress, House majority leader Jim Wright of Texas reported that drugs were draining $230 billion a year from the national economy. A federal bill was passed similar to the New York State Rockefeller Drug Laws. It ordered the death penalty for drug crime lords. It forbade probation or suspended sentences for those convicted of drug crimes. It authorized one billion dollars to build prisons. Another billion went to state and local narcotics squads. It repealed the exclusionary rule, which said prosecutors could not present evidence that had been obtained illegally.

MINORITY VICTIMS

The mood of the country was reflected in a 1987 statement by Justice Thurgood Marshall. "I ain't giving no break to no drug dealer," the justice said flatly.[10] As the only African-American member of the Supreme Court, Justice Marshall was echoing the widespread horror of the black community at the crack epidemic growing in the inner cities.

Throughout the 1980s and into the 1990s, crack took a heavy toll on minorities. Many unemployed young black men were attracted to drug dealing as a way to make money. They sometimes became role models for the children in their neighborhoods, who too often bought crack from them. Addiction to crack reached epidemic proportions in the inner cities. It spread to women as well as men. Soon so-called crack babies—babies who had been exposed to and had become addicted to crack in the womb—were being born.

With crack came violence. Turf wars broke out among dealers. Innocent people were wounded and killed. Young dealers and users came into schools and brought the violence with them.

OFF WITH THEIR HEADS!

Soon after George Bush was elected president in 1988, he put William Bennett in charge of the War on Drugs. By the end of Bennett's first year on the job, an 800 percent increase of people arrested for selling or producing heroin or cocaine was reported for the period between 1980 and 1989. In 1990, Bennett told talk-show host Larry King that "I don't have any problem" with beheading drug dealers.[11] With about 17 percent of high-school seniors using drugs—mostly marijuana—every month, Bennett's hard line was not unpopular.

In 1991 a Harvard University survey challenged the ongoing DEA claim that marijuana had no legitimate medical use. It offered evidence that pot can alleviate the nausea caused by chemotherapy in cancer patients. Also, doctors were suggesting it could block the wasting syndrome, which robbed AIDS patients of their appetites.

President Bush, however, was focused on the problem of drugs, not their medicinal value. In 1992 he announced the federal "Weed and Seed" program, which aimed to "weed" out neighborhood drug dealers and then "seed" the neighborhoods with education programs and social services. It was the kind of

The poor were the victims of the violence brought about by the crack epidemic. Ghetto minorities and their spokespersons were now the ones pleading the loudest for the government to devote more resources to the War on Drugs.

program minority communities welcomed. But Weed and Seed died when George Bush lost that year's election to Bill Clinton.

THE DRUG WAR CONTINUES

President Clinton appointed Joycelyn Elders to the post of surgeon general. In December 1993, Ms. Elders told the National Press Club that she thought it was possible the crime rate might go down if drugs were legalized, adding that the question needed studying. Her remarks brought a storm of criticism and contributed to the pressure that resulted in the president firing her.

Since then the war on drugs has been pursued on all fronts. Throughout the first Clinton administration the budgets for various War on Drugs programs were increased regularly. Yet a 1996 study by the University of Michigan's Institute for Social Research found that "daily [marijuana] use among eighth graders *quadrupled* since 1992."[12]

Nevertheless, the DEA claims that the War on Drugs is being won. A 1996 study by the Substance Abuse and Mental Health Services Administration seems to bear this out. It found that "an estimated 12.8 million Americans were current illicit drug users" as compared with 25 million in 1979.[13]

If drug use has been cut in half, however, concern over it has not decreased. In December 1997, *Newsday* reported that "30 national organizations representing more than 50 million people" had formed an alliance to fight drug use among young people.[14] They promised to devote one million hours of volunteer time to the project. There was to be no halt in the War on Drugs.

the case for reforming drug policy

Yes? No? Maybe?

"We Believe the Global War on Drugs Is Now Causing More Harm Than Drug Abuse Itself." That was the half-page headline of a two-page ad in *The New York Times* on June 8, 1998. The heading was followed by a letter to United Nations Secretary-General Kofi Annan. The letter pointed out that "U.N. agencies estimate the annual revenue generated by the illegal drug industry at $400 billion . . . roughly 8 percent of total international trade." It blamed crime, corruption, and violence on "decades of failed and futile drug war policies." It pleaded for a reexamination of global drug policies in which "punitive prohibitions yield to common sense, science, public health, and human rights."

The letter was signed by many prominent people around the world. More than 150 of them were citizens of the United States. They included the following: former Secretary of State George Shultz; author and broadcast journalist Walter Cronkite; federal Judge Whitman Knapp; Episcopal Bishop (retired) Paul Moore, Jr.; former New York City Police Commissioner Patrick Murphy; Harvard University professor and scientist-author Stephen Jay Gould; Executive Director of the American Civil Liberties Union Ira Glasser; economist Melvin Krauss of the Hoover Institution; former U.S. Surgeon General Joycelyn Elders; University of Pennsylvania Law Professor Lani Guinier; former Manhattan Borough President Ruth Messinger; San Francisco Mayor Willie Brown; Reverend Floyd Flake; Baltimore Mayor Kurt Schmoke; and author and Harvard University Professor Cornel West.[1]

A VARIETY OF POSITIONS

The debate over reforming drug policy begins with statistics. The figure of 12.8 million American users of illegal drugs—a 50 percent decrease over 17 years—is acknowledged by the DEA. The National Institute on Drug Abuse (NIDA) estimates that between 50 and 60 million Americans have used illegal drugs at some time. Advocates of drug-law reform say both figures raise a key question: Should such large groups of citizens really be considered lawbreakers?

As was pointed out in Chapter One, not all of these advocates want to legalize all drugs. Many support "decriminalization, not legalization—an important distinction." They believe in "moving addiction and drug problems away from the police and prisons and placing them in the hands of doctors and public health officials."[2]

There are other distinctions. Some people want to legalize only marijuana. Some want to provide heroin addicts with maintenance doses. Some want to put a stop to U.S. global drug policies because they believe they are hurting us internationally. Some are concerned with the costs of policing drugs and imprisoning users, some with the burden on the courts, some with the civil rights of those caught up in the War on Drugs, and some with the heavy sentences imposed for relatively minor drug offenses.

SOME JUDGES REBEL

Judge Whitman Knapp, who signed the letter to the UN secretary-general, is one of three federal judges who announced they would no longer preside over drug cases.

Putting people in jail for using drugs, according to Judge Knapp, wasn't doing any good. Judge Jack B. Weinstein and Judge Vincent L. Broderick, a former New York City police commissioner, agreed with Judge Knapp.

The heavy sentences judges are forced to hand down according to the federal statute modeled on the Rockefeller Drug Laws are, many believe, counterproductive. Juries are reluctant to convict young, small-time drug dealers when they know the law says they will have to go to jail for long periods of time. Prosecutors resent not being able to plea-bargain, and so they reduce the charges before they go into court.

WAR ON MINORITIES

Champions of minorities protest that African-Americans and Latinos make up an overwhelming majority of those affected by harsh drug laws. A 1990 Rand Corporation study found that over a three-year period 99 percent of defendants in drug trafficking cases in the United States were members of minority groups. More recently, a 1997 report by Human Rights Watch reported that in New York State "94 percent of people in prison under the Rockefeller Drug Laws are minorities."[3]

The African-American community resents the frequency of street sweeps in the inner cities, and of stop-and-frisk operations in which police detain and search innocent black youths. Some black and Latino leaders see a pattern in which minority drug users are arrested while white suburbanites who come to their neighborhoods to buy drugs are rarely bothered.

They are also outraged by the increase of narcotics raids in major cities. "They call it 'booming,'" a New York City police officer explained. "That's crashing the door down. . . . They boom the door and totally trash the apartment, but a lot of times they'll come up with nothing."[4] In late February and early March 1998, New York City police drug squads staged four botched raids in which innocent black people were terrorized.

POLICE VULNERABILITY

Municipal police departments across the nation have been damaged by the War on Drugs, according to critics. The huge sums of money involved in drug dealing have corrupted officers on the beat, narcotics squads, and even entire precincts. On the front line in a war they don't believe they can win, the police too often succumb to temptation.

Bribery is not the only police problem. Some officials believe that since the burden of enforcement has shifted to local departments while the federal government concentrates on stopping the drugs entering the country, police ability to fight other crime has suffered. "Crime does not go down when you take addicts off the street," says a New York City police captain. "In fact, there is some evidence that [crime] increases, that the preoccupation with addicts lets more serious criminals act more freely."[5]

The federal government has made it profitable for police departments to concentrate on drug-related crimes more than on other crimes. Under the law that allows the seizure of property of suspected drug dealers, there is a provision for participation by local police agencies. In many cases "80 percent of the assets [seized] are returned to the local police agency." According to an article in *The Nation* magazine, "as of 1994 the Justice Department had transferred almost $1.4 billion in forfeited assets to state and local law-enforcement agencies."[6] For some underfinanced police departments, the money from drug raids is a key part of their budgets.

ALL ABOUT MONEY

Money is also a major issue of the War on Drugs for those who oppose it. If drugs were decriminalized, they say, much of the $50 billion spent annually by federal and state government agencies might be used in such critical areas as health care, education, low-cost housing, and programs to reduce dependency on drugs and alcohol. There might even be funds left over for police departments that are short of money.

68

The War on Drugs, critics point out, has placed a great financial burden on prosecutors, public defenders, and the court system, which is backed up with untried cases. Defendants in those cases are often imprisoned for months while they await trial. According to a report released by drug czar General Barry R. McCaffrey, state and federal "governments spend $7.8 billion a year [on the] 80 percent of adults in U.S. prisons [who] are there for crimes related to drug and alcohol abuse."[7]

Mainly due to drug-related convictions, the prison population tripled to 1.7 million inmates between 1980 and 1996. Institutions can't hold the large numbers serving time for drug crimes. Many states are spending millions of dollars to build new prisons while their school buildings are crumbling.

Nobel Prize-winning economist Milton Friedman believes that "legalization would eliminate the immense profits earned by international drug cartels, street-drug dealers, and corrupt officials." In addition, "repealing laws against the manufacture, sale, and use of drugs would reduce violent crimes like theft and murder as it did when Congress repealed the prohibition against alcohol."[8] This too would save money for the criminal justice system.

DECRIMINALIZATION

Arnold Trebach, professor of criminal justice at American University in Washington, D.C., and director of the Drug Policy Center, takes a hard look at the NIDA figure of 50 to 60 million illegal drug users in the United States He points out that this indicates that "approximately one fourth of the U.S. population uses an illegal drug at least once a year." In his view, the War on Drugs is therefore "a war on 25 percent of the American people."[9]

Not all of these people, however, are addicted to—or even dependent on—the substances they use. Professor Trebach points out that "all drugs—including alcohol, tobacco, heroin, cocaine, PCP, marijuana—are dangerous. At the same time, all can be used in relatively non-harmful ways by many people.

The difficulty arises when people find they can't get along without these chemical crutches."[10]

He believes in decriminalization in which "all drugs could remain illegal." There would, however, be no prosecution for drug crimes not related to other crimes. In the future, however, Professor Trebach is convinced that "we must consider *full* legalization."[11]

Milton Friedman recommends "treating drugs as we now treat alcohol and tobacco: prohibiting sales of drugs to minors, outlawing the advertising of drugs, and similar measures." He adds that if the money that is now spent criminalizing drugs "was devoted to treatment and rehabilitation . . . the reduction in drug usage and in the harm done to the users could be dramatic."[12]

Proponents of drug-law reform suggest many strategies for dealing with the control and distribution of drugs. As with liquor, state boards might oversee sales, control prices, and mete out stiff penalties for selling to minors and other infractions of the rules. Users would not be punished, but as with cigarettes, there would be government-mandated campaigns to warn them against the use of drugs. Marijuana parlors might be licensed, just as bars and taverns are. Those who favor such approaches don't claim to have all the answers, but they do believe that any problems that arise can be handled and the benefits in terms of reduced drug-related crime make the effort worthwhile.

THE MARIJUANA CAMPAIGN

Much of the fight for outright legalization of drugs centers on marijuana. The National Organization to Reform Marijuana Laws (NORML) has long led this battle. NORML "supports the legalization of marijuana (hemp) for recreational, medicinal, and industrial use."[13]

NORML and its supporters insist that marijuana is far less harmful than tobacco and alcohol, which are sold legally. They cite scientific evidence showing that marijuana is not addic-

This 1995 Washington, D.C., rally to legalize marijuana uses a well-known drug-education acronym, DARE, to get its point across. In its original form, DARE stands for Drug Awareness Resistance Education.

tive. They challenge the gateway theory that says that smoking marijuana leads to using hard drugs. A study by the Institute of Medicine, a branch of the National Academy of Sciences, which was released in March 1999, confirms their claim that marijuana use does not lead to using heroin, cocaine, or other hard drugs.

In his book *Smoke and Mirrors: The War on Drugs and the Politics of Failure,* former *Wall Street Journal* reporter Dan Baum points out that if marijuana were legalized, "there wouldn't be 11 million regular [monthly, as defined by the FDA] users of illegal drugs in the United States, there would be 2 million."[14] In other words, nine million people who use only marijuana would no longer be using an *illegal* drug. Money, police power, and rehabilitation could then be concentrated on these hard-drug users.

THE MEDICAL BATTLE

Battles are also being fought over the medical use of marijuana. California voters approved legalization of marijuana for medical purposes in 1996. That same year Arizona voted to allow the use of marijuana in treating various illnesses. The federal government has been fighting to close California marijuana clubs, and has said it would prosecute doctors who prescribed marijuana, as well as establishments that sold it, even if they were filling doctors' prescriptions. Despite this, in 1998 measures allowing medical marijuana use were enacted in Alaska, Oregon, Nevada, and Washington State. All these measures contradict federal law.

Nevertheless, in California the battle for medical use of marijuana has attracted support from local officials, city councils, and mayors. They rarely hassle the marijuana clubs, which have defied federal attempts to shut them down. According to *The New York Times,* "about 10,000 ailing Californians are thought to buy marijuana for medical use." These include AIDS sufferers, cancer and chemotherapy patients, people with muscular sclerosis, those with glaucoma, and those who use it to "combat depression."[15] They include people of all economic levels, ethnic backgrounds, and ages.

"I have been using marijuana every day for the last six years," testified a 78-year-old grandmother who suffers from glaucoma. Puffing on her pot pipe at the San Francisco Cannabis Cultivators Club, she added that "it keeps the pressure down in your eyes. I also use it for arthritis."[16] The March 1999 Institute of Medicine study confirmed that marijuana appeared to be useful in relieving pain, nausea, and the severe weight loss associated with AIDS.

PROGRAMS UNDER ATTACK

Another major issue in the argument over drug policy is needle-exchange programs (NEPs), which focus on such dangerous hard drugs as heroin and crack. Mainlining these substances is common, and addicts routinely share needles. NEPs "provide sterile needles to addicts and encourage them to seek treatment."[17] Advocates are engaged in an ongoing battle against new laws prohibiting such programs.

Yet another program under attack is methadone treatment. Methadone is the drug given to heroin addicts, which satisfies their craving without causing the harmful effects of heroin. The use of methadone is opposed by New York City Mayor Rudolph Giuliani, who is phasing out methadone treatment centers. Advocates for methadone claim that it allows "users to function and sometimes to overcome their addictions."[18]

Campaigns against methadone clinics, medical marijuana, and needle-exchange programs are part of a new zero-tolerance strategy in the War on Drugs. This strategy—aimed at children even more than adults—teaches that there are no legitimate uses for illegal drugs and that they are always deadly. It has aroused opposition from a wide range of local groups, which include advocates for legalization, those for various programs of decriminalization, and people who simply feel that such a hard-line approach is unrealistic, sends the wrong message, and just doesn't work.

*Advocates of needle-exchange programs (NEPs)
say that there is evidence that these programs can
significantly slow the spread of AIDS, and that they do not
encourage increased drug use. A worker in Vancouver,
British Columbia, collects used syringes in that city's NEP.*

In Oakland, California, roughly a thousand anti-drug-war activists, community officials, and providers of services to drug users attended a 1997 national conference to consider harm reduction as an alternative to zero tolerance. The emphasis was on "prevention and treatment," as well as encouraging "more moderate use, safer use, the use of less dangerous drugs," and goals such as crime reduction and improving physical and mental health. One of the groups attending was the Oregon-based Mothers Against Misuse and Abuse, which believes that young people and children should be taught "basic drug consumer safety."[19]

Indeed, the battle between those who would reform drug laws and those who would strengthen the existing ones begins with the question of just what message should be given to the youth of the country. This chapter has provided one set of opinions on how that question should be answered. The next chapter will offer a very different—and opposing—set of views.

the case against reforming drug policy

Survey after survey shows that the War on Drugs has wide support among the American people. While this does not mean that they oppose all of the various proposals for reform and decriminalization that have been suggested, according to *The New York Times* columnist A. M. Rosenthal, "87 percent of Americans are against legalization."[1]

Every president since the late 1960s has approved the War on Drugs, and the elected and appointed officials in their administrations have pursued its goals. Across the country, the great majority of state and local officials and police departments have worked to stamp out drugs. Those involved in the struggle regard legalization as surrender just when the war is being won.

One of the most outspoken opponents of decriminalizing drugs is former drug czar William J. Bennett. "Law enforcement is not a political option or a policy question; it is a moral imperative," he insists. "The good guys must confront the bad guys and they must win."[2]

The late ex-President Richard Nixon, who launched the War on Drugs in 1968, wrote, in 1990, in favor of zero tolerance of illegal drugs. He advocated "total war . . . war on all fronts against an enemy with many faces." He pointed out that the enemy in this war is the casual user as well as the drug baron. He insisted that "*any* tolerance of *any* use of *any* illegal drug is wrong." Nixon regarded "calls for legalization of drugs [as] totally misguided."[3]

EASE OF PURCHASE

The logic is basic for those who oppose legalization. If drugs were legalized, they would be cheaper to buy and more easily available. As a result, more people would start using them. In particular, more children would be at risk.

As an example, they point to the legal selling of liquor since 1934 when Prohibition ended. Within ten years "per capita consumption in the United States rose from 0.97 gallon (3.7 liters) to 2.07 gallons (8 liters). (Today it is 2.25 gallons [8.5 liters].) If illicit drugs were suddenly legalized," they ask, "might not consumption similarly rise?"[4]

The comparison is of particular concern because of the rise in binge drinking among teenagers and the carnage on the highways caused by drunken drivers. Common sense says that legalizing drugs would make such problems worse.

If drugs were as easily available as alcohol, how could they be kept out of the hands of young people?

Opponents of legalization regard the proposals for licensing the sale of drugs and prohibiting drug sales to children as unworkable. They point to the ease with which young people can buy beer and wine coolers in grocery stores, bodegas, and supermarkets. They cite increased rates of smoking among children and believe that would occur with marijuana as well as tobacco cigarettes.

HARMFUL EFFECTS OF MARIJUANA

When it comes to marijuana, critics take issue with the argument that it is far less harmful than alcohol or tobacco. It is not true, they say, that smoking a couple of marijuana joints a day is no more harmful than smoking a pack of legal cigarettes containing nicotine. They raise "many disturbing questions about marijuana's effect on the vital systems of the body, on the brain and mind, on immunity and resistance, and on sex and reproduction."[5]

Those against both decriminalizing and/or legalizing marijuana refer to a University of California study showing that "the respiratory burden in smoke particulates and absorption of carbon monoxide from smoking just one marijuana joint is some four times greater than from smoking a single tobacco cigarette."[6] The study showed that one puff of marijuana inflicted three times the amount of tar on the mouth and lungs as a puff from a filter-tip cigarette. Carbon monoxide levels were four to five times as high.

The Center for Psychological Studies in New York City found that ongoing marijuana use distorted users' perception of how they were functioning. Smokers felt as if they were dealing with work and relationship problems better, but in reality the marijuana was often blocking them from dealing with these problems at all. The conclusion was that a "feel-good" solution such as marijuana was, actually, no solution.

CRACK: AN INNER-CITY PLAGUE

Arguments against legalizing and/or decriminalizing marijuana may draw support from concerned parents, but it is usually professionals in the War on Drugs who make them. It's different with crack. The staunchest opponents of its decriminalization are those who must deal with its effects on a daily basis.

These are the people who live in the poor neighborhoods of the inner cities. They are the ones whose children are most likely to be lured into using crack at an early age. Crack is the drug that afflicts the poor and minorities most. It is more dangerous than other drugs because it is sold on the street by floater dealers (many of them addicts themselves) who come and go and who have little control over the quality of what they are selling. Crack is relatively cheap compared with pure cocaine, and because impurities are common, they may add to the anguish and increase the chances of death. Addicts are a blight on the community, and some of them have not even reached their teens yet. Babies born to addicted mothers are addicts themselves.

Harlem Congressman Charles Rangel says that the black community is losing its children to drugs. He believes that legalization would create more addicts and more problems. Do we just say that the War on Drugs is lost and hand our children over to the crack dealers, he wonders.

The Drug Enforcement Administration rejects the pro-legalization argument that drug-related violence is the result of crack dealers' turf wars, which would cease if the drug was decriminalized and regulated. The DEA claims that "most drug violence is committed by people under the influence of drugs."[7] They believe that legalization would increase family violence, child neglect, and social-welfare costs in the inner cities.

GETTING TOUGH ON COCAINE

While crack cocaine is the plague of the inner cities, cocaine that is not freebased is considered "the champagne of drugs, the high-class high, a status symbol of the rock star, the movie queen, the best-selling author." This description is from *Cocaine: The Great White Plague* by Dr. Gabriel G. Nahas, Ph.D. He is firmly against making cocaine legal. "The use of cocaine in a society," Dr. Nahas writes, "is a sign of its confusion and decline; it is the door open to self-destruction. It is high time that social taboos be restored against the great addicter."[8]

Dr. Nahas's views reflect the fact that law enforcement is not evenhanded when it comes to cocaine. It is sniffed mostly in the privacy of the home in middle- and upper-class areas where other crime rates are low compared with the inner cities. The police do not usually concentrate their limited resources on drug use in such areas.

Cocaine, however—like marijuana—is often bought on inner-city streets. As Dr. Herbert Kleber pointed out in the *New England Journal of Medicine,* "the illegal, open-air drug bazaars that flourish in southeastern Washington, D.C., and the South Bronx would not be tolerated in Georgetown or Scarsdale [New York]."[9] This discrepancy between how the drug war is fought in poor urban areas and well-off suburbs concerns those who oppose legalization.

It is time, they believe, to start vigorously prosecuting those otherwise upright citizens who use cocaine. They are the ignored links in a chain, which begins with the international drug cartels, winds through the violence and crime of drug dealing in the United States, and too often results in antisocial acts by cocaine users themselves and their children.

These children learn by example. Mom and Dad break the law. *They snort snow, so why shouldn't we smoke pot?* How much worse might the results of these messages be if cocaine and marijuana could be bought legally?

HEROIN: OPTIONS AND OPPOSITION

Although cocaine and marijuana use involves many times as many people as heroin does, it is the idea of legalizing heroin that most outrages opponents. That addicts would legally "be able to purchase the heroin and needles they need at reasonable prices" strikes them as "absurd." So too does the proposal that heroin users enter maintenance programs, which would supply the drug to them in measured (but not increased) doses. "Heroin," they say, "is no cure for heroin addiction."[10]

Many of them extend their opposition to needle-exchange programs. Harlem Hospital's Director of Psychiatry James L. Curtis says flatly that "there is no evidence that such programs work." He insists that "needle exchanges merely help addicts continue to use drugs."[11] The Clinton administration decided not to fund such programs.

However, there is a division among drug legalization opponents regarding methadone treatment. Drug czar Barry

McCaffrey believes it works and asks why in the world anyone would recommend heroin maintenance over methadone maintenance. New York City Mayor Rudolph Giuliani, however, argues that "methadone maintenance programs simply substitute one dependency for another, and that abstinence from drugs is a more moral and decent approach to curing addiction."[12]

Dr. Mitchell Rosenberg, president of Phoenix House, a network of drug treatment centers that don't use methadone, thinks the mayor is on the right track. Citing "the large number of people who are really stuck and not making progress," Dr. Rosenthal believes the mayor "may be making a real contribution to rethinking this aspect of public policy."[13]

VICTORY FOR SATAN

Many of those in the front lines of the War on Drugs agree with Mayor Giuliani that the issue of drugs is basically one of morality. Like Representative Tom Petri who opposes any pullback in the drug war, they see drug use as a legacy of the 1960s, "part of the counterculture, of the [Vietnam] antiwar movement, of rebellion against authority."[14] They believe that any use of drugs is basically immoral, and that widespread drug use is evidence of a breakdown of the American way of life.

In particular, they view drugs as an assault on family values. They identify them with ills affecting the family, such as extramarital affairs, divorce, wife battering, child abuse, and others. They believe drugs are related to a lack of parental discipline, disrespect by children, premarital sex, and out-of-wedlock births.

They consider legalizing drugs to be the equivalent of opening the doors of their homes to immorality and evil. "One of the least understood aspects of the drug problem is the degree to which it is in the end a moral and spiritual problem," said former drug czar William Bennett.[15] Many religious leaders of varying faiths—from the metropolitan inner cities to the rural plains of mid-America—agree that the struggle with drugs is between God and the Devil, and that legalization would be a victory for Satan.

DO DRUGS, DO TIME!

In some places the moral revulsion toward drugs has resulted in hard-line legislation and prosecution. This is the case in Maricopa County, Arizona. Here County Attorney Richard M. Romley concluded that casual drug users were "responsible for a large portion of the demand for illegal drugs in this country."[16] He enlisted twenty-six local, county, state, and federal law-enforcement agencies in the Maricopa County Demand Reduction Program.

The purpose of the program is to reduce the demand for illegal drugs by cracking down on occasional users. Its slogan is "Do drugs, do time!" County Attorney Romley has found it to be "an effective deterrent in our war on drugs."[17] Other localities across the country have adopted similar programs.

Such hard-line approaches may be a backlash against those who advocate legalization, decriminalization, or harm reduction campaigns. In particular, the hard-liners do not see the logic in the so-called "compromise of harm reduction," which "does not seek to get people off drugs but merely to help them use drugs more safely." They see no way in which harm reduction can "bring down the appallingly high levels of drug addiction in this country."[18]

THE HIDDEN COSTS OF DECRIMINALIZATION AND LEGALIZATION

Those against any programs that go easy on illegal drugs insist that the cost of the War on Drugs has been money well spent. According to the DEA, a "1994 Household Survey on Drug Abuse demonstrates unequivocally that drug use declined significantly between 1979 and 1994."[19] The most recent Monitoring the Future Study conducted by University of Michigan research scientists for the U.S. Department of

Health and Human Services shows that marijuana and hashish use among high-school seniors decreased from 33.7 percent in 1980 to 19 percent in 1994. While there has been a slight rise in marijuana use since 1994, this may be a short-term effect due to growth and diversity in the high-school population. Over the long term, marijuana use, like other illegal substance use, will continue to decrease according to those who champion the War on Drugs.

They point out that the portion of the U.S. budget spent fighting illegal drugs is tiny compared with that spent on other programs, and that the sum becomes truly insignificant when one considers that "drug abuse costs the United States between $60 and $100 billion in lost productivity each year."[20] They challenge the idea that money saved by discontinuing the War on Drugs could then be spent on education, welfare, drug rehabilitation, and other social programs.

Legalization would cost more in their view than the War on Drugs does. The increase in drug use that would result would cause across-the-board expenses to society. There would be the cost of regulating legalized drugs, of ensuring their purity, of monitoring and licensing growers, importers, and dealers. There would be an additional financial burden on schools and police charged with seeing that drugs did not fall into the hands of minors. Legalization would trigger "lost workplace productivity and a resultant increase in the cost of goods."[21] Drug treatment costs would mount. More users would commit more crimes, and prison costs would rise.

Finally, those against repealing the drug laws wonder why we would deal with what they consider to be illegal, and possibly immoral, activity by condoning it rather than prosecuting it. Barry McCaffrey points out that "many advocates of harm reduction consider drug use a part of the human condition that will always be with us." But, he adds, "while we agree that murder, pedophilia, and child prostitution can never be eliminated entirely, no one is arguing that we legalize these activities."[22] Why then, should we legalize harmful drugs?

a global problem

Yes? Maybe? No?

Given the United Nations estimate of $400 billion spent every year on illegal drugs, the question is, just how is such a vast amount spent? Huge profits are involved, but how are they generated? How does the yield of a flower like the opium poppy become so valuable?

In seeking answers, the Asian country Burma (now known as Myanmar) is a good place to start. Two pounds (1 kilogram) of raw opium grown there sells for "$66 to $75." The same kilo of "prepared morphine base on the Thai border" goes for "$900 to $1,000." As "refined heroin," the kilo fetches between $6,000 and $10,000 in Bangkok. By the time it reaches U.S. shores, the "wholesale refined heroin cost" is "$90,000–$250,000 per kilo." Finally, "adulterated street sale of cut heroin in the United States, if calculated by the kilo, [is] $940,000–$1,400,000."[1]

As of November 1996, opium from Burma accounted for two thirds of the heroin seized by law-enforcement agents on U.S. streets. Illegal drug earnings, often invested in legitimate business enterprises, were equal to Burma's entire earnings from legally exported goods and services. In 1997, "Burma produced an estimated 2,600 tons of opium, [which is] enough to make more than 200 tons of heroin—at least 60 percent of the world total."[2]

Burma is a major part of the Golden Triangle, an area of opium fields, which includes sections of Laos and Thailand. According to Pino Arlacchi, executive director of the United Nations International Drug Control Program, progress has been made in lowering opium production in the Golden Triangle. Drug warlords have struck deals with the new military government in Burma, which let them keep their freedom and money in exchange for backing away from the merchandising of opium. Arlacchi points out that "Thailand has virtually eliminated opium production."[3]

ALTERNATIVE DEVELOPMENT

Pino Arlacchi "advocates so-called alternative development programs that would induce opium and coca growers to switch to less profitable legal crops by bringing roads, hospitals, schools, and a better life into remote rural areas that depend on drug crops to survive."[4] In Peru alternative development helped reduce the output of coca (the source of cocaine) by 40 percent in two years. Bolivia promised to stop growing coca within five years.

Drug czar Barry R. McCaffrey, although supportive of Arlacchi's efforts, has some doubts about whether alternative development can work. His reservations may be based on statements made by leaders and spokespersons of some of the drug-producing countries themselves. In nations like Colombia, Mexico, the Dominican Republic, and Turkey, the drug trade is so tied to the national economy that cutting back on production or distribution threatens these countries' financial stability.

The people of the world have shown that they want drugs, say those who protest how the War on Drugs impacts on their countries. If that is a problem for the United States, let them deal with the demand within their own boundaries. The United States, they say, has no right to try to change the agricultural patterns or trade of other nations. If drugs are against the law in the United States, then prosecute the users and dealers there; don't harass poor farmers and merchants in other countries.

TROUBLE WITH MEXICO

The War on Drugs has caused much friction between the United States and Mexico. A large part of the interdiction money allocated by Congress is spent on the U.S.-Mexican border. In February 1998, President Clinton proposed employing an additional one thousand border patrol officers. The only objection from Republicans in Congress was that there should be more.

The United States also supplies money and materials directly to Mexico for the War on Drugs. However, the General Accounting Office (GAO) concluded that "planes, helicopters, and ships sent to Mexico by the United States have largely been inoperable, inadequate, or ineffective in the drug fight."[5] For instance, seventy-two UH-IH Huey helicopters given to Mexico had to be grounded because the Mexican government found that they were unsafe.

In 1997, U.S. customs agents seized "607,000 pounds (275,578 kilograms) of marijuana and 46,000 pounds (20,884 kilograms) of cocaine"[6] on the border. The drugs were concealed in truck tires, automobile axles, fuel tanks, and inside hollowed-out vegetables in crates. U.S. intelligence reports have labeled the Mexican police as corrupt. They have also implicated high-ranking Mexican government officials in the drug trade.

However, ordinary Mexican citizens in border areas protest that U.S. drug-enforcement agents are high-handed and don't respect the sovereignty of their country. They say that they are subjected to unreasonable body searches when they cross the border to work on the United States side, while tourists from the United States coming into Mexico simply walk across.

THE CERTIFICATION QUESTION

In order to receive financial help from the United States to fight the War on Drugs, countries must be certified as cooperative by the president. In 1997, President Clinton certified Mexico. Members of Congress objected. The Mexican drug czar had just been arrested for his involvement with a top drug dealer. Mexico was "a primary transit route for cocaine, and a major producer of heroin, methamphetamines and marijuana."[7] Nevertheless, the certification of Mexico stood and was renewed in 1998.

Colombia, however, was not certified in 1997 and in 1998 received only conditional certification. This means that War on Drugs activities in Colombia—"where some 80 percent of the cocaine sold in the United States originates"—will be carefully monitored in the future.[8] Nevertheless, in the late 1990s, aid to fight drugs in Colombia increased from $22 million to $100 million.

According to a 1997 report by the GAO, aid to Colombia has "made little impact on the availability of illegal drugs in the United States." In fact, "the total area [in Colombia] under coca cultivation rose nearly 20 percent." It may be relevant that U.S. officials accuse Colombian President Ernesto Samper of financing his election with drug money.[9]

RESULTS IN COLOMBIA

Colombia's economy has been fueled by cocaine. Some years back, drug traffickers circulated throughout the rural areas of the country and distributed seed and fertilizer to grow coca. They gave guarantees to the farmers that they would buy the crops. It was a boon to the growers, doubling and sometimes tripling their incomes. They describe it as a joyride, and call it "La Bonanza."[10]

The United States fought this practice by paying Colombian pilots to dust the coca crops with poison. Nearly 99,000 acres (40,063 hectares) of coca crops were destroyed in 1998. Randall Beers, U.S. acting assistant secretary for International Narcotics and Law Enforcement Affairs, described the program as "the most cost-effective way to reduce narcotics substances."[11]

Once, the most powerful forces in Colombia were the drug cartels. The Medellin cartel and the Cali mafia, as they were known, directed "a vast global network of cocaine production, transportation, wholesale distribution, and money-laundering operations." At one time they were said by the DEA to "export hundreds of tons of cocaine into the United States annually." However, by the late 1990s the seven top leaders "[had] either been arrested or [had] surrendered to Colombian authorities." The DEA considers this to have broken the power hold of the Colombian drug cartels.[12]

NEW DRUG PROVIDERS

The problem is that as crackdowns on growers and drug traffickers succeed in one area, production and distribution shift to other areas. One of those concerned with stopping drugs before they reach the shores of the United States, Coast Guard Vice Admiral Roger Rufe, Jr., explains it this way: "When you press the balloon in one area, it pops up in another. It's a market economy; with demand as it is in the United States, they have plenty of incentive to try other routes."[13]

Distribution routes have shifted to the Caribbean. Between 1996 and 1997, there was a 100 percent increase in cocaine reaching the United States from the Caribbean. Inside the United States, particularly in the northeast, control of the drug trade has shifted from Colombia, Mexico, and Cuba to the Dominican Republic. "The Dominicans are our biggest threat" according to New England DEA Regional Director George Festa. However, Moisés Pérez, a Dominican-American spokesperson, points out that the number of Dominicans in the

As the growing of illegal drugs is reduced in such areas as the Golden Triangle, their cultivation increases in countries like Pakistan and Nigeria. Poor farmers do better with poppies and coca than with food crops. New distributors take over as many top drug lords are forced out of the business. This Afghan farmer inspects his crop near the Pakistani border.

United States who are involved in the drug trade is small "when you compare it to the size of the community."[14]

Once, the big question was how to stop the drug trade. Today more and more people around the world are asking what can be done to reduce the worldwide appetite for drugs. Other countries are trying different ways of dealing with that problem. Their successes—and failures—may point the way for the United States.

other countries, other programs

Yes? No? Maybe?

The two countries with the most controversial drug programs are Switzerland and the Netherlands. Both have experimented with harm reduction and decriminalization. In turn, both have been praised and condemned for their permissive approach to drugs.

The Netherlands in particular has drawn criticism from neighboring countries who claim that lax prosecution of narcotics cases has created a safe haven for European drug dealers. From the Netherlands, they say, illegal drugs flow across the borders of France, Belgium, and Germany. The Dutch take the complaints seriously and are tightening some of their drug policies.

CONCERN FOR THE YOUNG

Dutch drug policies stem from the Revised Opium Act enacted by the Dutch Parliament in 1976. The act made a strong distinction between hard drugs (heroin) and soft drugs (marijuana). The drug policy that evolved from the act treated marijuana "as a relatively innocent substance suitable to be used for pleasure and recreation."[1]

The main aim of the policy, according to the Netherlands Institute of Mental Health and Addiction, "is to protect the health of individual users, the people around them, and society as a whole." This is different from the United States' priority of ending, or at least greatly reducing, drug use and trafficking. The Dutch policy gives priority "to young people in particular."[2]

Authorities act "on the principle that everything should be done to stop drug users from entering the criminal underworld [and so] the use of drugs is not an offense."[3] Rather than punishing young marijuana smokers, the emphasis is on keeping them away from prisons and other places where they might encounter hardened criminals or be introduced to hard drugs. The Dutch Ministry for Welfare and Public Health finds that "alcohol and tobacco give more reasons for concern than cannabis [marijuana]."[4]

THE COFFEE SHOPS

Indeed, marijuana is, under some circumstances, made available to Dutch high-school students because that is considered better than punishing them with suspensions or expulsions from school, or having them buy it illegally. Marijuana is discussed as a health topic in Dutch classrooms. The intent is to inform teenagers about the risks involved and to stress that, like alcohol, it should only be used moderately.

Young people who smoke marijuana are urged to do so in coffee shops that openly sell the drug. There are rules governing these coffee shops. They are not allowed to sell alcohol or hard drugs. They may dispense no more than five grams of marijuana or hashish in any single transaction. Drugs may not be advertised. The shops must not cause any nuisance to local neighborhoods.

Theoretically, they may not sell drugs to anyone under the age of eighteen. That works out no better in the Netherlands than does the prohibition against selling cigarettes to minors in the United States. So long as they behave, the underage marijuana users who frequent the coffee shops are not hassled.

A young man lights a bong, or water pipe used for smoking marijuana, inside a coffee shop in the Dutch city of Amsterdam.

DUTCH GOVERNMENT CLAIMS SUCCESS

The coffee shops, along with treatment centers and methadone clinics for heroin addicts, attest to the permissive nature of Dutch drug policy. The question is, how well does it work? The answer depends on who is asked.

The Netherlands Institute of Mental Health and Addiction believes that it is working well compared with the programs of other European countries. They report "2.4 drug-related deaths per million inhabitants in the Netherlands in 1995. In France this figure was 9.5, in Germany 20, in Sweden 23.5 and in Spain 27.1."[5] The increase in marijuana use is no greater than the increase in other countries. The number of Dutch heroin addicts—25,000—has not changed in many years.

More significantly, the policy of separating marijuana smokers from hard-drug users seems to have worked. Today there are relatively few young heroin addicts in the Netherlands. The average age of heroin addicts is thirty-three, indicating that marijuana has not been a gateway drug for young pot smokers.

NOT EVERYBODY AGREES

Some Dutch experts do not agree that the permissive policies have been successful. Dr. Ed Leuw cites a national survey of sixteen- and seventeen-year-olds that showed an increase in marijuana use "from 6 percent in 1988 to about 13 percent in 1992."[6] He blames this on the availability of pot in coffee shops.

He also sees evidence that more young marijuana users have become dependent on the drug. Dr. Leuw points out that while "in 1988, 1.2 percent of all admissions into addiction care were primarily for cannabis [marijuana] use, in 1995 this proportion had increased to 4.5 percent."[7] This means that there had been an increase of more than two thousand marijuana addiction admissions.

94

Such statistics focus suspicion on the coffee shops. Many of them are located in poor urban neighborhoods. Some people who frequent them may be peddling hard drugs to young customers. More likely, they are selling hard drugs to the tourists who visit the coffee houses. Some of these drugs end up back in the tourists' native countries—a fact that has drawn strong protests from France, for example.

Also, there is a criminal element that frequents the coffee houses to size up possible robbery victims high on pot. The Dutch government denies that the country's crime rate has risen, but residents of poorer neighborhoods believe it has, and they blame the coffee houses. In response to their claim, the government cut back on the number of coffee houses allowed to sell marijuana. Even so, the majority of Dutch citizens approve their government's permissive drug policy.

NEEDLE PARK

Switzerland's lenient drug policies are for the most part also approved by that country's citizens. Here, although hemp—the source of marijuana—is freely grown in rural areas, both soft and hard drugs are mainly urban problems. When votes are taken at the municipal level, overwhelming support is shown for harm reduction programs over punitive measures. In Zurich on December 1, 1996, voters approved a program that gives heroin to hard-core addicts by a margin of 63 percent to 37 percent.

Heroin became a problem in Zurich in the early 1980s. By 1986 the drug scene had settled in the Platzspitz—widely known as "Needle Park." There were an estimated three thousand heroin addicts camped out there.

Authorities tolerated Needle Park as a place where people could use drugs without being arrested. The police believed that it was better to have the addicts all shooting up in one place rather than scattered around the city. As the AIDS threat grew, free needles were distributed by the municipal authorities in Needle Park.

Despite the efforts of municipal authorities to keep the drug use in Needle Park safe, the death rate there tripled over five years. This led to the permanent closing of the park in 1995.

The park, however, became a magnet for heroin users from all over Europe. Freedom from the threat of arrest and the needle-exchange program drew them there. With them came rival drug dealers and violence. Police closed down Needle Park in 1992, then allowed it to reopen, and finally closed it for good in 1995.

SWISS GOVERNMENT DEALS DRUGS

In 1994 the Swiss government began "selling heroin to hard-core users." It was "an experiment to determine whether prescribing heroin, morphine, and injectable methadone will save Switzerland both money and misery by reducing crime, disease, and death." Cities were given the option of taking part in the experiment. Most did. In Basel, when those opposed to it forced a vote, "65 percent of the electorate approved a local heroin prescription program."[8]

There are differences in the programs from city to city. Some provide only methadone, while others offer a choice of cocaine and heroin, marijuana cigarettes, and "sugarettes" (tobacco cigarettes injected with heroin). Some cities have so-called street rooms where intravenous heroin injections are allowed. These are supervised to prevent drug dealing on the premises. Other cities have strictly regulated methadone programs in which clients use a magnetized card to draw a dose of methadone into a cup. Careful records are kept of daily dosages. This prevents overdoses and the resale of methadone on the black market.

SUCCESS OR FAILURE?

How successful are these programs? The Zurich Social Welfare Department found that "heroin prescription is feasible, and has produced no black market in diverted heroin [and that] the health of the addicts in the program has clearly improved." The Social Welfare Department concluded that "heroin per se causes very few, if any, problems when it is used in a controlled fashion and administered in hygienic conditions." Those who administered the programs "also found little support for the widespread belief that addicts' cravings for heroin are insatiable." Many who had increased their dosages voluntarily cut them back to a maintenance level.[9]

These conclusions are challenged by Youth Without Drugs, a Swiss organization that campaigns for a policy of abstinence. The organization would do away with controlled drug use and methadone programs. It makes no distinction between hard and soft drugs, and wants stiff narcotics laws and strong police enforcement.

Dr. Ernst W. Aesbach, a member of the Board of Youth Without Drugs, views needle distribution and methadone programs as having removed "any motivation for drug addicts to quit using drugs." He points out that "50 percent of participants of abstinence-based programs live without consuming drugs" for at least two years, while that is only true of "42.4 percent of methadone recipients." He deplores the closing of facilities in which "coercive withdrawal" was used to end drug addiction.[10]

Dr. Aesbach also cites various studies showing increases in Swiss marijuana use, particularly among young people. Finally, he points out that Swiss drug programs are in violation of the Principle Guidelines on Demand Reduction adopted by the General Assembly of the United Nations. The goal of abstinence from drug use is a key principle of those guidelines.

OTHER EUROPEAN COUNTRIES

Despite disapproval, the Swiss experiments in providing drugs to users are being copied in other countries, including Denmark, Luxemburg, and Australia. In Spain drug use is not unlawful, although there are fines for using drugs in public places. Norway distributes clean needles to heroin addicts and concentrates its resources on the treatment of users rather than on enforcement of antidrug laws.

Italy repealed a 1975 law that said that "the personal use of drugs is not a legal offense."[11] Greece takes a contradictory line, offering legal approval for treatment of drug offenders, but not providing treatment programs. In Israel, where drug use by young people is a growing problem, the Anti-Drug Authority (ADA) spends half of its budget on treatment. The Palestinian Authority conducts its own drug education program for schoolchildren and older students.

THE MIDDLE EAST AND AFRICA

Throughout the Middle East, countries serve as transshipment points for illegal drugs. However, the prevailing Muslim religion is a powerful deterrent to the use of drugs (including alcohol). In large cities like Cairo, Egypt, where the religious influence is not quite as strong, hashish is the drug of choice. Egypt has severe laws against drug use, but it also offers a drug-awareness program, which targets school-age children. In Syria drug use is extremely low, and the government seizes the assets of anyone involved in the drug trade. The United Arab Emirates (UAE) imposes harsh sentences for drug possession and puts drug traffickers to death.

Many African countries also transship illegal drugs. However, they do not have domestic drug-use problems on the scale of those in the United States and Europe. Marijuana is grown and widely used domestically in most African nations, but this is not as much of a problem as the flow of hard drugs in and out of these countries.

The African drug trade has resulted in a rise in drug abuse in Nigeria, which lacks the resources to deal with the problem. Kenya has laws against growing marijuana, but they are not strongly enforced, and pot smoking is on the upswing among young people. There is also a problem with drug dealers recruiting European and American tourists as couriers. In Ghana there is increasing use of cocaine and heroin despite the efforts of regional narcotics squads to crack down on both users and dealers. In Botswana farmers depend on revenue from marijuana crops, which are consumed locally. In Liberia drug-related arrests are increasing in the midst of a civil war. Mozambique does not have a serious drug abuse problem, although marijuana use is deeply embedded in rural culture. In Zimbabwe, consumption of heroin, Ecstasy, and methamphetamines (speed) has increased; Zimbabwe has no national drug policy, but there is a drug squad that cracks down on users and dealers at the street level.[12]

ECSTASY IN SCOTLAND

Zimbabwe is only one of many places where the designer drug Ecstasy has gained popularity. Because of its unproven reputation as a love drug, which enhances sex, the appeal of Ecstasy crosses cultural lines as well as national boundaries. Even more than in Zimbabwe, it is catching on in England and Scotland.

The unpredictable effects of Ecstasy have led dance clubs in Glasgow and Edinburgh to establish so-called chill-out areas. When Ecstasy combines with strenuous dancing and the high temperatures in many clubs, it can cause dehydration and heatstroke. Despite this, chill-out areas are opposed by the Glasgow, Scotland, Licensing Board.

Still, the Licensing Board does little but express its opposition. That is not unusual in Great Britain, which has a history of ambivalence toward drugs. Great Britain is still subject to the 1971 Misuse of Drugs Act, which makes distinctions between drug possession and drug dealing, as well as between soft drugs and hard drugs. It also allows doctors to prescribe hard drugs.

DISSENSION IN ENGLAND

This causes controversy in Cheshire, England, where Dr. John Marks gives pure heroin to known addicts. His reasoning is that it would keep them from performing criminal acts to support their habit. Many of the addicts claim that Dr. Marks has changed their lives, turning them into functioning and self-supporting citizens. Opponents, however, believe that Dr. Marks simply plays into their addiction.

Dr. Marks is beyond the reach of the law. In Great Britain, that is not unusual. According to Mike Trace, director of Great

Britain's Prisoners Resource Service, "the vast majority of drug possession offenses are now dealt with by a police warning that does not even involve a court appearance."[13]

CREW 2000

In Edinburgh, Scotland, where heroin use skyrocketed in the late 1980s and early 1990s, a harm reduction program was introduced. Needle-exchange programs reduced the spread of AIDS, and free counseling and methadone cut back on shoplifting and mugging by heroin addicts. However, the results proved not to be lasting. Today a younger generation of Scots are turning to heroin as an antiestablishment gesture. Even some former addicts now say that harm reduction only perpetuates addiction.

A group called Crew 2000 has sprung up in Edinburgh to confront the drug problem. They provide confidential advice and information on drugs to users. Their data are based on interactive, up-to-date drug databases. They give referrals for counseling and provide clubs with a chill-out service, which includes guidelines for safer dancing, temperature control, and emergency treatment. They try to be factual, nonjudgmental, and not moralistic in their approach.

Their bottom line is expressed in their slogan: *Drugs: The only way to avoid the risk is not to use them.*[14] That may be advice worth thinking about.

afterword

We have seen that drugs are a global problem as well as a national problem. We have seen examples of zero tolerance, crackdowns on users and dealers, efforts to stop drugs at the source, and interdiction strategies to stop international trafficking. We have looked at harm reduction campaigns, needle-exchange programs, educational efforts, methadone distribution, decriminalization, and legalization attempts. We have learned about successes and failures in all these approaches.

To some, the problem of drugs and the questions that surround it are moral issues. To some they are matters of law. To some they are health problems. To some they are concerns of individual liberty. To some they are economic questions, and to others they are issues of life and death.

All of these points of view are valid. In accepting any one of them, however, it is important to regard drugs from the other standpoints. Too many of the arguments are based on emotion rather than on hard facts. To come to grips with the issues means coming to grips with all sides of them.

Weigh the evidence. Consider the cost of drugs to society. Look at the expense of the War on Drugs. Consider both in terms of human suffering as well as financial burdens. Should drugs be legalized? You decide.

chronology

400 B.C.	Hippocrates prescribes high doses of opium for many ailments.
Early 1800s	British East India Company monopolizes China drug trade.
1839–1842	Opium Wars: China vs. England, France, and the United States.
1858	Treaty of Tientsin legalizes China opium trade.
1861–1865	Approximately 400,000 soldiers are addicted to morphine, a form of opium, during the U.S. Civil War.
1886	Coca-Cola containing cocaine comes on the market.
1903	Coca-Cola removes cocaine from its products.
1909	Importing and possessing opium outlawed in the United States.
1912–1914	The Hague Convention ratifies worldwide regulation of opium.

1914	Harrison Narcotics Act regulating marketing of drugs is passed by Congress.
1919	Prohibition becomes law in the United States.
1920	League of Nations takes over supervision of opium and other dangerous drugs.
1933	Prohibition is repealed.
1937	Congress passes the Marijuana Tax Act.
1945	U.S. border patrols seize record amounts of marijuana.
1968	Republican presidential candidate Richard Nixon launches the War on Drugs.
1969	Woodstock Festival focuses attention on drugs.
1970	Authority over drugs is transferred from the U.S. surgeon general to the attorney general. National Organization for the Reform of Marijuana Laws (NORML) is formed.
1970–71	Congress provides funds for methadone treatment centers.
1971	The United States gives Turkey $35 million to destroy its opium crop.
1973	New York State legislature passes the Rockefeller Drug Laws.
1978	New federal law allows the Drug Enforcement Agency (DEA) to seize money and property of suspected drug dealers.
1979	Crack epidemic begins.
1980	DEA launches campaign for state laws to outlaw drug paraphernalia.

1982	*Toughlove*, a book advocating hard-line approach toward kids on drugs, hits best-seller lists.
	National Academy of Sciences study finds marijuana not addictive.
1984	First Lady Nancy Reagan launches "Just Say No!" campaign.
1986	President Ronald Reagan orders federal agencies to test employees for drug use.
	Congress passes tough legislation based on New York's Rockefeller Drug Laws.
1988	William Bennett named "drug czar" by President George Bush.
1991	Harvard University study concludes marijuana has valid medical uses.
1992	President Bush announces "Weed and Seed" program.
1993	Surgeon General Joycelyn Elders says question of legalizing drugs should be studied.
1996	University of Michigan study finds that marijuana use among eighth graders quadrupled over four years.
1997	U.S. Coast Guard seizes 51.8 tons of cocaine.
1998	United Nations Secretary-General Kofi Annan reports the existence of more than 50 million drug abusers worldwide.
	President Clinton announces next federal budget will contain $17 billion for War on Drugs.

source notes

chapter one

1. Christopher S. Wren, "At Drug Summit, Clinton Asks Nations to Set Aside Blame," *The New York Times*, June 9, 1998, p. A6.
2. Christopher S. Wren, "Drugs or Alcohol Linked to 80 percent of Inmates," *The New York Times*, January 9, 1998, p. A14.
3. Author uncredited, "Study Finds Parents Lack Facts About Marijuana," *The New York Times*, April 13, 1998, p. A16.
4. Wren, "At Drug Summit, Clinton Asks Nations to Set Aside Blame," p. A6.
5. Eric Schmitt, "Drug Czar Tells of New Efforts as Clinton Trumpets Successes," *The New York Times*, December 12, 1997, p. A32.
6. Ibid.
7. Eric Blumenson and Eva Nilsen, "The Drug War's Hidden Economic Agenda," *The Nation*, March 9, 1998, p. 16.

chapter two

1. *Grolier Multimedia Encyclopedia*, 1998 Edition.
2. Ibid.
3. Ibid.

4. Helen Cordes, "Generation Wired," *The Nation*, April 27, 1998, p. 12.
5. Ibid.
6. Jean Carper Food Pharmacy, "Red Wine Outdoes White Wine in Battle Against Cholesterol," *The Denver Post*, October 11, 1995, p. F04.
7. *Grolier Multimedia Encyclopedia.*
8. Ibid.
9. Author uncredited, *Alcohol: An Inquiries Guide* of the American Heart Association, 1998, p. 1.
10. *Grolier Multimedia Encyclopedia.*
11. Michael Massing, "Strong Stuff," *The New York Times Magazine*, March 22, 1998, p. 38.
12. Jane Gross, "Young Blacks Link Tobacco Use to Marijuana," *The New York Times*, April 22, 1998, p. B7.
13. Ibid.

chapter three

1. *Compton's Interactive Encyclopedia,* 1998 Edition.
2. Ibid.
3. *Grolier Multimedia Encyclopedia*, 1998 Edition.
4. Gabriel G. Nahas, M.D., Ph.D., *Cocaine: The Great White Plague* (Middlebury, VT: Paul S. Eriksson, 1989), p. 109.
5. Ronald K. Siegel, Ph.D., "Chemical Dependency Is Instinctual," *Chemical Dependency: Opposing Viewpoints* (San Diego, CA: Greenhaven Press, Inc., 1991), p. 18.
6. Ronald K. Siegel, Ph.D., *Intoxication: Life in Pursuit of Artificial Paradise* (New York: E. P. Dutton, 1989), p. 154.
7. Ibid., p. 157.
8. Ibid., p. 160.
9. Ibid., p. 130.

chapter four

1. *The Holy Bible* (New York: Oxford University Press, 1950) p. 9.
2. Ronald K. Siegel, Ph.D., *Intoxication: Life in Pursuit of Artificial Paradise* (New York: E. P. Dutton, 1989), p. 260.

3. Ibid.
4. Siegel, p. 144.
5. *Encyclopaedia Britannica, 15th ed., Macropaedia* (Chicago: Encyclopaedia Britannica, Inc., 1984), vol. 5, p. 1053.
6. Ibid.
7. Siegel, p. 269.
8. *Encyclopaedia Britannica,* p. 1051.
9. Siegel, p. 270.
10. Carl Sifakis, *The Encyclopedia of American Crime* (New York: Facts On File, Inc., 1982), p. 519.
11. Sifakis, p. 590.
12. Siegel, p. 273.
13. Dan Baum, *Smoke and Mirrors: The War on Drugs and the Politics of Failure* (Boston: Little, Brown and Company, 1996), p. 50.

chapter five

1. Dan Baum, *Smoke and Mirrors: The War on Drugs and the Politics of Failure* (Boston: Little, Brown and Company, 1996), p. 12.
2. Baum, p. 8.
3. *Encyclopaedia Britannica, 15th ed., Macropaedia* (Chicago: Encyclopaedia Britannica, Inc., 1984), vol. 5, p. 1052.
4. Clifton Daniel, editor in chief *Chronicle of the Twentieth Century* (Mount Kisco, NY: Chronicle Publications, 1987), p. 1005.
5. Baum, p. 25.
6. Baum, p. 152.
7. Baum, p. 200.
8. *Plague* (New York: DC Comics, 1983), cover.
9. Baum, p. 216.
10. *Life* magazine, Fall 1987, p. 109.
11. Baum, p. 298.
12. Daniel R. Levine, "Drugs Are Back Big Time," in *Substance Abuse,* ed. Joseph Sora (New York: H. W. Wilson Company, 1997), p. 51.

13. *Drug Use in the United States,* DEA Publications Briefing Book Internet release, p. 1.
14. Author uncredited, "Drug Fight Pledged," *Newsday,* November 19, 1997, p. A26.

chapter six

1. *The New York Times,* June 8, 1998, pp. A12–A13.
2. Harry G. Levine, "Prisons Aren't Answer," *The New York Times*, April 18, 1998, p. A12.
3. Jennifer Gonnerman, "New York's Drug Law," *Village Voice*, May 12, 1998, p. 45.
4. Bob Herbert, "A Cop's View," *The New York Times Week in Review,* March 15, 1998, p. 17.
5. Dan Baum, *Smoke and Mirrors: The War on Drugs and the Politics of Failure* (Boston: Little, Brown and Company, 1996), p. 81.
6. Eric Blumenson and Eva Nilsen, "The Drug War's Hidden Economic Agenda," *The Nation,* March 9, 1998, p. 12.
7. Nancy A. Youssef, "Help Urged for Inmate Addicts," *The Chicago Tribune,* January 9, 1998, p. 20.
8. Charles P. Cozic and Karin Swisher, ed., *Chemical Dependency: Opposing Viewpoints* (San Diego, CA: Greenhaven Press, Inc., 1991), p. 132.
9. Arnold Trebach, "Illegal Drug Use Should Be Decriminalized," *Chemical Dependency: Opposing Viewpoints* (San Diego, CA: Greenhaven Press, Inc., 1991), p. 152.
10. Trebach, p. 153.
11. Trebach, p. 155.
12. Ibid.
13. NORML Statement of Policy from natlnorml@aol.com.
14. Baum, p. 332.
15. James Brooke, "Moving to Semantical High Ground," *The New York Times,* March 1, 1998, p.18.
16. Ibid.
17. Eva Bertram and Kenneth Sharpe, "Resisters Say We're Fighting the Wrong Battles," *The Nation,* January 6, 1997, p. 13.

18. Ibid.
19. Ibid.

chapter seven

1. A. M. Rosenthal, "Lean Back or Fight," *The New York Times,* April 14, 1998, p. A19.
2. William J. Bennett, "Law Enforcement Efforts Should Be Increased," *Chemical Dependency: Opposing Viewpoints* (San Diego, CA: Greenhaven Press, Inc., 1991), p. 160.
3. Richard Nixon, "Zero Tolerance for Drugs Can Reduce Chemical Dependency," *Chemical Dependency: Opposing Viewpoints* (San Diego, CA: Greenhaven Press, Inc., 1991), p. 232.
4. Michael Massing, "Winning the Drug War Isn't So Hard After All," *The New York Times Magazine*, September 6, 1998, p. 48.
5. James A. Inciardi and Duane C. McBride, "Illegal Drugs Should Remain Illegal," *Chemical Dependency: Opposing Viewpoints* (San Diego, CA: Greenhaven Press, Inc., 1991), p. 144.
6. Ibid.
7. DEA: "Speaking Out Against Drug Legalization, Claim X, Drug Legalization Would Have an Adverse Effect on Low-Income Communities," www.usdoj.gov/dea/pubs/legaliz/claim19.htm.
8. Gabriel G. Nahas, M.D., Ph.D., *Cocaine: The Great White Plague* (Middlebury, VT: Paul S. Eriksson, 1989), p. 119.
9. DEA: "Speaking Out Against Drug Legalization, Claim X..."
10. Barry R. McCaffrey, "Legalization of Drugs Wrong, Regardless of How It Is Done," *The Houston Chronicle*, August 2, 1998, p. 4.
11. James L. Curtis, "Clean But Not Safe," *The New York Times,* April 22, 1998, p. A 27.
12. Rachel L. Swarns, "Giuliani Acts to Withdraw Methadone from Addicts," *The New York Times,* August 15, 1998, p. A13.
13. Ian Fisher, "Drug Drive Has Little Chance, Experts Say," *The New York Times,* July 22, 1998, p. B6.

14. Tom Petri, "We Must Renew the War on Drugs," www.house.gov/petri/weekly/aug29col.htm.
15. Bennett, p. 235.
16. Richard M. Romley, "Do drugs. Do time," www.maricopa.gov/attorney/dddt.html.
17. Ibid.
18. Massing, p. 49.
19. DEA: "Speaking Out Against Drug Legalization, Claim II, We Have Made Significant Progress," www.usdoj.gov/dea/pubs/legaliz/claim02.htm.
20. DEA: "Speaking Out Against Drug Legalization, Claim VIII, Drug Control Spending Is a Minor Portion," p.2, www.usdoj.gov/dea/pubs/legaliz/claim08.htm.
21. DEA: "Speaking Out Against Drug Legalization, Claim II..., p. 1."
22. McCaffrey, p. 4.

chapter eight

1. Jonathan Spence, "In Xanadu," *The New York Times Book Review,* July 26, 1998, p. 9.
2. Christopher S. Wren, "Where Opium Reigned, Burmese Claim Inroads," *The New York Times,* April 19, 1998, p. 8.
3. Christopher S. Wren, "U.N. Aide Would Fight Drugs With a Better Life for Growers," *The New York Times,* June 7, 1998, p. 5.
4. Ibid.
5. Tim Golden, "Study Faults U.S. Military Aid Sent to Mexico's Anti-Drug Effort," *The New York Times,* March 19, 1998, p. A5.)
6. Sam Howe Verhovek, "Trade Pact Brings Drug Searches and Traffic Jams," *The New York Times*, March 20, 1998, p. A12.
7. Eva Bertram and Kenneth Sharpe, "The Drug War's Phony Fix: Why Certification Doesn't Work," *The Nation,* April 28, 1997, p. 18.
8. Diana Jean Schemo, "Colombian Peasants Seek Way Out of Drug Trade," *The New York Times,* February 28, 1998, p. A1.
9. Schemo, pp. A1 & A5.
10. Schemo, p. A1.
11. Schemo, p. A5.
12. DEA Internet Briefing Book, *Major Traffickers and Their*

Organizations, www.druglibrary.org/schaffer/idea/pub/briefing/
2-8.htm.
13. Bertram and Sharpe, p. 21.
14. Clifford Krauss and Larry Rohter, "Dominican Drug Traffickers
    Tighten Grip on the Northeast," *The New York Times,* May 11,
    1998, p. A1.

chapter nine

1. Ed Leuw, "Dutch Soft Drug Policy in Theory and Practice,"
   Internet position paper, Netherlands Ministry of Health, Welfare
   and Sport,www.thc.nl/documents/leuw%20dutch %20soft
   %20drugs%20pol...
2. "Dutch Drugs Policy," Internet Fact Sheet, Trimbos Institute
   [Netherlands Institute of Mental Health and Addiction], voor-
   lichting@best-dep.minjust.nl, p. 1.
3. Ibid.
4. Leuw, www.thc.nl/documents/leuw%20dutch %20soft%20
   drugs%20pol...
5. "Dutch Drugs Policy," Internet Fact Sheet.
6. Leuw, www.thc.nl/documents/leuw%20dutch%20soft%20
   drugs%20pol...
7. Ibid.
8. Ethan A. Nadelmann, "Switzerland's Heroin Experiment,"
   National Review, July 10, 1995, p. 46.
9. Nadelmann, pp. 46–47.
10. Ernst W. Aesbach, M.D., "Flawed Swiss Drug Policy," testi-
    mony at the Senate caucus on International Narcotics Control,
    Internet, June 18,1998, www2.druginfoorg/orgs/dsi/intpolicy/
    flawedswissdrugpolicy.html, pp. 3, 4, 5.)
11. R. Bricolo, M.D., "Italy: The Drug Laws," Internet position
    paper, www.penlex.org.uk/italy.html, p. 1.
12. Note: All data on Middle Eastern and African countries are from
    the U.S. Department of State, *International Narcotics Control
    Strategy Report, March 1997,* www.state.gov/www/global
    /narcotics_law/1997_narc_report/index.html.
13. Mike Trace, "Great Britain: The Drug Laws," www.penlex.
    org.uk/britain.html.

14. Crew 2000 Internet information sheet, crew20000@electric frog.co.uk.

Note: *Due to the changing nature of Internet sites, sources used in writing this book may no longer be available online. A Web search by subject will lead you to the latest information available.*

organizations to contact

CREW 2000, 32/32a Cockburn Street, Edinburgh, Scotland, EH1 1PB. Phone: (0131) 220-3404.

Drug Enforcement Administration (DEA), Information Services Section (CPI), 700 Army-Navy Drive, Arlington, VA 22202. Phone: (202) 401-7834. Museum (open Tuesdays–Fridays, 10 A.M. to 4 P.M.) Museum phone (202) 307-3463.

Parents Resource Institute for Drug Education (PRIDE), 3610 Dekalb Technology Parkway, Suite 105, Atlanta, GA 30430. Phone: (770) 458-9900.

Partnership for a Drug Free America, 405 Lexington Avenue, New York, NY 10174. Phone: (212) 922-1560.

Partnership for Responsible Drug Information, 14 West 68th Street, New York, NY 10023. Phone: (212) 362-1964.

Phoenix House Foundation Inc., Drug Education and Prevention Unit, 33 West 60th Street, New York, NY 10023. Phone: (212) 787-3000.

Substance Abuse 24-Hour Helpline and Treatment (Address Confidential), Phone: 1-800-234-0420.

United Nations International Drug Control Programme, Vienna International Centre, PO Box 500, A-1400, Vienna, Austria. Phone: +43-1-26060 0.

internet sites

(All have links to related sites.)

Carl E. Olsen's Marijuana Archive—mojo.calyx.net/-olsen
Drug Enforcement Administration (DEA)—www.usdoj.gov/dea/
Drug Reform Coordination Network—www.stopthedrugwar.org
Federal Information Exchange—web.fie.com
National Academy of Sciences—www.nas.edu
National Institute on Drug Abuse—www.nida.nih.gov
National Organization for the Reform of Marijuana Laws (NORML)—norml.org
Prevline–National Clearinghouse for Alcohol and Drug Information—www.health.org
U.S. Department of Health and Human Services—www.os.dhhs.gov

further reading

Baum, Dan. *Smoke and Mirrors: The War on Drugs and the Politics of Failure* (Boston: Little, Brown and Company, 1996).

Bender, David L., and Bruno Leone, eds. *Chemical Dependency: Opposing Viewpoints* (San Diego, CA: Greenhaven Press, Inc., 1991).

Bennett, William J. *The De-Valuing of America: The Fight for Our Culture and Our Children* (New York: Simon & Schuster, 1992).

Booth, Martin. *Opium: A History* (New York: St. Martin's Press, 1998).

Nahas, Gabriel G., M.D., Ph.D. *Cocaine: The Great White Plague* (Middlebury, VT: Paul S. Eriksson, 1989).

Sharp, Elaine B. *The Dilemma of Drug Policy in the United States* (New York: HarperCollins, 1994).

Siegel, Ronald K., Ph.D. *Intoxication: Life in Pursuit of Artificial Paradise* (New York: E. P. Dutton, 1989).

Sifakis, Carl. *The Encyclopedia of American Crime* (New York: Facts On File, 1982).

York, Phyllis, David York, and Ted Wachtel. *Toughlove* (New York: Doubleday, 1982).

glossary

Addict: one who is hooked on a drug and can't stop taking it

Addiction: a physical need to continue taking a drug

Amphetamines: drugs that stimulate

Angel Dust (PCP): particularly unstable hallucinogen

Booming: breaking down the door in police drug raids

Caffeine: a legal amphetamine

Coca: leaves of the coca bush; the source of cocaine

Cocaine: white powder made from coca leaves and usually sniffed to provide a short-term high

Courier: a low-level drug smuggler

Crack: cocaine that has been "freebased" and so is stronger and more dangerous

DEA: Drug Enforcement Administration; Justice Department agency charged with antidrug enforcement

Decriminalization: a wide range of programs designed to shift the focus on substance abuse from law-enforcement agencies to health and rehabilitation agencies, and to make drug use less subject to criminal law

Delirium Tremens (DTs): shakes and/or hallucinations resulting from excessive use of alcohol

Dependency: a psychological need to continue taking a drug

Ecstasy: a designer drug and hallucinogen, which has been rumored (without proof) to enhance sex

Freebasing: boiling crystals of cocaine in various solutions

Gateway drug: a so-called soft drug such as marijuana, which leads to the use of more dangerous drugs like crack and heroin

Grass: marijuana

Hallucinogens: mind-altering drugs, such as LSD, Angel Dust, and Ecstasy

Harm reduction: programs that seek to ease the damage to society and drug users rather than to stop the spread of drugs

Harrison Narcotics Act: passed in 1914, it called for "the orderly marketing of drugs" like cocaine and opium

Hashish: similar to marijuana, but much more potent

Hemp: the plant source of marijuana and hashish

Heroin: made from poppies; a strong narcotic that is particularly dangerous when mainlined (injected); extremely addictive

Interdiction: the policy of seizing illegal drugs en route from one country to another

Laudanum: a popular nineteenth-century medicine containing opium and sold over the counter without a prescription

Legalization: repealing drug laws—sometimes only marijuana statutes, sometimes laws against other drugs, or all drugs

Mainlining: injecting heroin, or any other drug, directly into a vein

Maintenance habit: drug use that increases neither the strength nor the amount of the substance taken

Marijuana: a product of the hemp plant; a so-called soft drug; the most commonly used illegal substance in the United States

Methadone: a synthetic drug used to wean addicts away from heroin

Morphine: processed from the same source as opium and heroin; it is widely used in hospitals as a painkiller

Needle-exchange program: giving new needles to addicts in exchange for used ones to stop the spread of AIDS and other diseases

Nicotine: the most potent—and harmful—ingredient in tobacco

NORML: National Organization for the Reform of Marijuana Laws

Opium: fruit of the poppy, which—unlike heroin—is usually smoked rather than injected

Pot: marijuana

Prohibition: the 1919 constitutional amendment that banned the sale of liquor in the United States; repealed in 1933

Rockefeller Drug Laws: New York State statutes mandating harsh sentences in drug cases; basis for later federal legislation

Speed: amphetamines

Steroids: drugs used to enhance athletic performance at the risk of undesirable—and sometimes dangerous—side effects

Tough love: the belief that parents should take a hard-line punitive approach to drug-using children

Tranquilizers: legal substances such as Valium and Librium that depress the central nervous system and relieve anxiety

Transshipment: moving illegal drugs through a third country while en route from the source country to the market country

Uppers: speed; amphetamines

User: one who uses drugs over a period of time but is not necessarily an addict

War on Drugs: the campaign launched by President Richard Nixon in 1968 "to fight the plague of drugs"; still official U.S. policy today

Water pipe: paraphernalia used to smoke opium

Zero tolerance: treating any and all use of illegal drugs as a crime and prosecuting users vigorously

index